CHAOS...
TO CRISIS…
TO CHRIST!

BY RANDALL H. ROGERS JR.

TABLE OF CONTENTS

ACKNOWLEDGMENTS

I would like to acknowledge with heartfelt gratitude the following people and their very valuable contributions to my life over the years. Without their support and prayers the writing of this book would not have been possible.

Dr. Ernest Franklin and his lovely wife Joyce who trusted me with their home repairs and gave me work doing my medical reconstruction. I will be forever grateful for the faith and love they extended to me in Christ Jesus that gave the courage to move forward to my destiny.

Dr. James A. Davis who played a very significant role in my coming back to a place of normalcy due to his tireless efforts acting as my agent seeking the expertise of other doctors that aided in my reconstruction. I will be eternally grateful for all his work on my mouth and nose and the sacrifices that he made towards me.

Dr. Thomas Osborne who provided me with titanium implants below cost along with in office surgeries in association with Dr. Davis. I am grateful for all that he was able to accomplish in the short time that we worked together.

Dr. Robert Wood who poured his heart and soul over into my recovery and labored to exhaustion in using every medical technique even the experimental that was available to him in my reconstruction. I'll never forget his labor of love.

Dr. Dostel who operated on me several times and whom God used to set His agreement in the spirit in the operating room, when I was unable to speak a single word that changed the course of my surgeries from failures to successes.

Dr. Stephen Cohen who did countless surgeries and most of the cosmetic surgeries in my reconstruction and was instrumental in helping me come to a place where I could use my mouth and speak and regain my place in society without the stigma of shame.

And all the Hospital staff at Grady Memorial Hospital, Northside Hospital, St. Joseph Hospital and Shallowford Hospital.

To Dave and Diana Hope who allowed me to design a waterfall and pond in their backyard during some of the worse depression that I have ever experienced. It made me feel needed in a small way that someone cared enough to trust me with a project that large.

To the dozens of Doctors who came from England, France, Germany, Spain, and Israel and from all over the world who played their part in my reconstruction whose names allude me now, but whose sacrifices will never be forgotten. For I wear their sacrifices and God given talents in my body daily.

To all those who came over from Emory University Medical Center.

To all the nurses, whose compassion and tenderness made my time in the hospital tolerable? They may be an overlooked and forgotten people, because their jobs may not seem to be of major importance as to rate acknowledgment, *but to me they are the most valuable and will never be forgotten.*

And they rate so say I.

And a very special acknowledgment to all the members of Christ Fellowship Church of Atlanta, whose prayers and words of encouragement blessed me in the darkest hours of my life. Their prayers were a comfort and a spiritual salve that travelled with me during my recovery and have continued over these many years in my ongoing healing.

In addition, I want to acknowledge all the loving and compassionate Registered Nurses at Newnan Hospital, who showed me the compassion of God in every way during my recent stay. My healing and my future health will be in no small part due to their passion and commitment to their professionalism. I pray the Lord's blessing on all of you, and may He give you His strength as you continue to help those who are sick and who cannot help themselves.

And finally, last but not least to my mother, who gave of the little that she had in helping me when I unable to help myself. The love a mother has for her only son is very special. A mother's love never changes towards her children, and I am thankful that she was there for me when I needed her the most.

I pray to my Father in heaven that all those who have helped me and touched my life over these many years that He will bless each and every one of you until you overflow with all the desires of your heart.

I ask in the Holy Name of Christ Jesus that each person that has touched my life be rewarded 100 fold in this life and in the life to come.

In the name of Christ Jesus I ask and pray...

DEDICATION

I have labored for quite some time as to the person to whom this book should be dedicated to. There are many people who are worthy and who have played a significant role in my spiritual development and maturity.

But after careful consideration, I have concluded that without the help of this one person I would not have even begun my journey to find the Truth, moreover I would never have come into the knowledge of the love of God, that has forever changed my life.

He was there with me when I was ordered to dig my own grave and He was with me when leaned I against that cold Georgia red clay and died emotionally. He saw my broken heart, and He has seen every tear that I have shed.

This person has been by my side night and day from the very beginning of my life. He has helped me through the darkest trials of my life constantly speaking words of encouragement and love. He has led me by paths that I was not familiar with, speaking gentle words of compassion urging me onward and upward to my destiny in Christ Jesus.

He has been closer to me than a brother and it is because of His tireless supernatural efforts that I stand now in this place of grace and mercy today.

He has never rebuked me or spoken a harsh word in anger even though so many times I am sure I warranted such words. His words were always filled with compassion and love as He spoke to me the words that He heard my Father in heaven speak.

This person has remained hidden in the background of my life and has spoken gently to me many times through a thin veil.

I speak of <u>"The Blessed Holy Spirit."</u>

"The writing of books there is no end and many books have been written by men as the Holy Spirit moved upon them. But few books have honored the Holy Spirit personally for all that He has done for them.

I therefore, hereby dedicate this book to him.

For by honoring, The Blessed Holy Spirit,

I honor my Father in heaven and my Lord Christ Jesus.

Opening Prayer
O God Most High, receive all the praises.

O God Most High, receive all the honour and glory.

For you, and you alone are worthy.

O God Most High, O Ancient One, may the words written here bring you great glory and honour and may your Blessed Holy Spirit touch the hearts of all who read these words in a deep and profound way.

May you, O Mighty One who sits on High, have access to your people and may you come forth in great power to awaken your people and bring revival in our nation. Set our hearts afire again and may we be a people of love and compassion sent to a lost and dying world.

Jesus hear my prayer, Jesus, hear my cry, look at my heart and let your mercy begin to fall like rain upon this nation as never before. Let your salvation shine forth and let all of your creation see your glory.

O Ancient One, hear my cry, hear my plea, hear my petition, and do not allow us to be destroyed along with those who do not believe. But in your great compassion have great mercy on your creation.

O God on high, let my words vibrate against your holy throne and may you be aroused to jealousy and come gather your inheritance.

Have mercy upon the United States of America!

Rise up, O Mighty One, and come in great power!

Let your salvation shine forth! Give us one last opportunity to return to our first love. Save Christ Jesus.

We want to see your Kingdom come! Let it come! Let it come! In the Name above all names, I ask in the name of Christ Jesus, Let it come.

CHAOS...
TO CRISIS...
TO CHRIST!

I AM THE WAY AND THE TRUTH AND THE LIFE. NO ONE COMES UNTO THE FATHER EXCEPT THROUGH ME. JOHN 14:6

PLEASE NOTE: ALL SCRIPTURAL REFERENCES ARE FROM THE NEW INTERNATIONAL VERSION AND MAYBE BE PARAPHRASE

<u>THIS IS MY DECLARATION OF THE TRUTHS THAT I HOLD DEAR IN MY HEART.</u>

<u>I BELIEVE IN THE ONE AND ONLY TRUE GOD.</u>

<u>THE GREAT CREATOR OF ALL THINGS.</u>

<u>I BELIEVE IN JESUS CHRIST THE ONLY BEGOTTEN SON OF GOD ALMIGHTY.</u>

<u>I BELIEVE THAT HE ROSE FROM THE GRAVE ON THE THIRD DAY BY THE POWER OF HIS FATHER IN HEAVEN.</u>

<u>I BELIEVE I HAVE BEEN WASHED IN HIS HOLY AND PURE BLOOD AND MADE RIGHTEOUS IN CHRIST JESUS.</u>

I BELIEVE THAT CHRIST JESUS IS SEATED IN HEAVEN AT THE RIGHT HAND OF HIS FATHER IN HEAVEN.

I BELIEVE THAT HE WILL SOON COME FOR ALL THOSE THAT HE DIED FOR AND WHO HAVE ACCEPTED HIS HOLY BLOOD ATONEMENT.

I BELIEVE I WILL BE AMONG THEM... I BELIEVE... IN CHRIST JESUS.

HE IS THE KING OF KINGS AND LORD OF LORDS.

HE IS THE GREAT I AM!

HE IS MY GOD. HE IS MY KING.

HE IS MY FRIEND...

MY FATHER IN HEAVEN LOVES ME, AND I LOVE HIM.

INTRODUCTION

Our lives here on earth are cast between the opposing forces of heaven and hell. We seem to be caught up in a giant chess game with the Great Creator on one side and the great destroyer on the other. We go from crisis to crisis never knowing why we are experiencing negative emotions, destructive behavior and the associated pain. Eventually, succumbing to the weight of the pressure inwardly we begin to think that in death we will find a place of rest. We have become weary with the mundane routines of this life and desire to escape at any cost physically and mentally.

Thoughts of suicide and self -medication begin to consume our every waking moment. We desire to numb the debilitating feelings of our pain, insecurities, failures and fears. We had become like walking corpses of decaying flesh existing above ground wondering aimlessly for our final resting spot. Thoughts of hopelessness and feelings of self-loathing mount as we sink ever deeper into the darkness of a self-created world of depression.

Yet, it is only at this dark place of the soul that we can hear the Good, the Glad, the Merry news, that causes a man to leap the dance for joy. It is only after we have come to the end of ourselves having exhausted all of our earthly options that we are ready to make a decision that will change the course of our life and our eternal destiny. It is only here that we are ready to walk the Valley of the shadow of death.

Psalms 23 1:6 The Lord is my shepherd, I shall not be in want. He makes me to lie down in green pastures, he leads me besides quiet waters, and He restores my soul. He guides me in the path of righteousness for his name's sake. Even though I walk through the valley of the shadow of death, I will fear no evil, for you are with me, your rod and staff, they comfort me. You prepare a table before me in the presence of my enemies. You anoint my head with oil, my cup overflows. Surely goodness and love will follow me all the days of my life, and I will dwell in the house of the Lord forever.

I am writing these words as a way of encouragement to those who now find themselves in this valley, or who have found themselves in this valley in the past with little or no understanding. There is hope and victory and wisdom at the end of this journey. The ways of God are beyond our thinking and yet, even the most simple minded among us can understand the ways of God, if we're willing to walk humbly before him in brokenness and humility.

Psalms 149:4 for the Lord takes pleasure in his people, he adores the humble with victory.

These following words come from many years of God dealing with me and my chaos and eventually bringing me into a deep revelation and a conscious awareness of his great and everlasting love for my soul. Isaiah 55: 8-9 "for my thoughts are not your thoughts, and neither are your ways my ways, as the heavens are higher than the earth, so are my ways higher than your ways, and my thoughts higher than your thoughts." Every human that has taken a breath from the fall of Adam has had one thing in common, "The Valley" for each person has been brought to walk through the Valley of the Shadow of Death. It is our failures and even our limited successes that eventually cause us to walk this valley. For every man must enter and walk this valley alone, for it is the prerequisite demanded of God unto salvation and eternal life.

Chapter 1

THE PRICE FOR TRUTH

For some, this will be a lifetime event for failing to understand and accept the ways of God in dealing with man. For some this journey will be repeated many times for failing to humble themselves in order that they might receive the wisdom and instruction in the ways of God. We live in a cruel and unforgiving world and coming into this Valley seems to be the last straw that breaks us into many pieces. It is our stiff backs and arrogant attitudes that has set us at odds with the Lord of hosts. For every soul that finds himself in this Valley has been led there by the Spirit of God for the express purpose of having the truth about Christ Jesus and his sacrifice upon the Cross of Calvary revealed to them in their inner most parts.

This journey will require brokeness, humility and contrition and will bring about a new way of living. Living for God, living a life of victory and overcoming the things that robbed us when we lived for ourselves. A life of true spiritual freedom, a life designed by God himself. For the life we live is through His only begotten Son for his glory his honor and his praise.

Psalms 51: 6 surely you desire truth in the inner parts, teach me wisdom in the inmost place.

As we enter the Valley of the Shadow of Death we come face to face with the image that we have created outside the knowledge of God. In our own eyes we enter clothed, but in spiritual reality we are clothed only in arrogance and rebellion to the ways of God. We find ourselves standing naked, wretched, blind and poor in this great darkness, having been brought in guilty before our Great Creator. We look for an escape but the valley walls are too steep and insurmountable even by human ingenuity and strength. We are weak and weary from striving to accomplish our agenda on earth. Yet in our little remaining strength we stand defiant and proud having tried to remodel our lives by what-ever means possible.

In our own eyes we stand proud filled with decep-tion and arrogance in our ways of thinking. In our futile attempts to direct our own life we have only succeeded in creating chaos and from that point we have moved from crisis to crisis affecting everyone and everything.

We have experienced great pain and suffering in our own lives and caused great pain in the lives of everyone we have come in contact with on our journey. The pain of our failures and loses that we have buried deep within our heart will never allow us to accomplish anything of eternal value or redemption. For what we bury alive remains alive.

Our internal appraisal of ourselves makes us question our very own existence. We question the reason over and over why were born and why are we still alive? We may seek to have the manifest reality of God in our lives, but inwardly resist the ordained ways of God to our own end. Living our lives here on earth without the revelation of Christ Jesus in our innermost parts is an attempt to exist on a survival level at best.

This truth will come at a high price to our self- life even crucifixion. For there can be no true manifest reality of the Spirit of God in the innermost parts of our being without traveling the same paths that our forefathers have taken before us. There must be a complete breaking of the old man before the new man created by God can emerge. For salvation means, the putting back together again of the pieces of a broken life.

We must be brought to a place of complete breakdown in order to see our breakthrough. We must be stripped of our every ability and strength to maintain and control our lives, so that the power of God which is all surpassing, can be our only sustaining source. It is here at this juncture and only here that we see our need for supernatural intervention in our lives to sustain our lives and carry us over into the place of victory. It is only here that we see our need for a Savior.

This then is the Valley of God, for the express purpose of God, that the sacrifice of His only begotten Son might be embrace completely by all those who enter. It is of God and for God and by God through Christ Jesus our Lord and Savior.

This is the great choice. This is the great decision. This is the Valley of Decision.

Much of our mental illnesses and physical diseases can be directly related to the chaos in the soul due to the rebellion of our thoughts through a mind that has not come under the submission of the Sovereign God. Our mental institutions are filled with people that have shut down their minds because of the rebellion and the unarticulated pain they carry in their soul. Spiritual and physical blindness is a direct result of looking for the answer to our problems within ourselves.

When we look within ourselves without acknowledging the Cross of Jesus Christ for the answer to our problems we will only find a dark void.

This is the pride, arrogance and ignorance of man. Ignorance is not an acceptable defense before God. To look within ourselves is to only find darkness and great frustration. Being in the Valley of decision is one of the tools that God uses to bring us to Himself. For God left this void for himself. Our rejection and denial of this truth will not change its reality.

Our destinies here on earth will be left unfulfilled and our eternal rewards will be left upon the table, if we resist the work of the Holy Spirit in the Valley of Decision. If we fail to humble ourselves here, we will live out our lives on planet earth in a senseless mediocrity, wandering aimlessly, powerless to overcome the trials of this life. We will never accomplish anything of value or eternal worthiness that will glorify our Creator and give us a sense of purpose and destiny.

Worse yet, we will never taste the sweet victory over the enemy of our soul. John 15:5 I am the vine and you are the branches, if a man remains in me and I in him, he will bear much fruit, apart from me you can do nothing.

It is the Spirit of God that allows the chaos in our lives in order to bring us to the great revelation of His son. This is the way of the Lord.

We will find our true identities and self-worth in Christ Jesus as we gaze into the eyes of the One and only True God.

It is only after have passed through this valley that we will exit into the glorious light of an all loving, all righteous and merciful God. We will be clothed in robes of His righteousness and His purity. And this by His great power.

For God is love.

And this by his grace.

We will be seated with Him to live a new life with his power manifesting in us and through us having overcome the world and all its temptation. Because we now know that we are in Him who overcame the world before us, so that we by his grace we will do good works for His glory, His honor and His praise. We now have a purpose to live and the power to accomplish this directive from God. For now we know that we are no longer enemies of God because by His great grace and by His decision from before the foundations of the earth, we have been accepted in the Beloved, and we are now friends of God.

Ephesians 2:1-10 as for you, you were dead in your transgressions and sins, in which you used to live when you follow the ways of the world and the ruler of the kingdom of the air, the spirit who is now at work in those who are disobedient. All of us also lived among them at one time, gratifying the cravings of our sinful natures and following its desires and thoughts. Like the rest, we were by nature objects of wrath. But because of his great love for us, God, who is rich in mercy, made us alive in Christ even when we were dead in our transgressions-it is by grace you have been saved. And God raised us up with Christ and seated us with him in the heavenly realms in Christ Jesus, in order that in the coming ages that he might show the incomparable riches of his grace express in his kindnesses to us in Christ Jesus.

For it is by grace you have been saved, through faith, and this not of yourself, it is the gift of God-not by works, so that no man can boast. For we are God's workmanship, created in Christ Jesus to do good works, which God has prepared in the advance for us to do.

This identification is necessary for our eternal life as well as for our calling to return to edify those who are ready to make the journey into the Valley of Decision. We return to encourage those yet to enter the valley with these words, having ourselves experienced the tender mercies of this loving God first hand.

We are led to this Valley and begin our journey because we are thirsty for that which will truly satisfy our longings and refresh our soul. It is here in our decision that we are allowed to drink from the quiet waters, and our soul needs nothing more, for we come in hungry and we are fed with the bread of life. And we are satisfied. We are satisfied with life itself.

Even Christ Jesus...

We come in unloved, betrayed and lost and we are bathed in the everlasting love of God Almighty. And our soul desires nothing more.

For we are satisfied. For He becomes our foundatation of life.

We find him who now has become our everything. Our living source. . .

We find the lover of our soul.

John 6:35 I am the bread of life. He who comes to me will never go hungry, and he who believes in me will never be thirsty.

We find our Heavenly Father.

Your chaos is for God!

The crisis situation that you now find yourself in is your heavenly father wooing you unto himself. For He will lead you into the Valley of decision where you will find rest for your weary soul and pure water to satisfy your thirst. There you will meet the life giver himself and partake of His body and of his precious holy blood unto salvation and eternal life.

You will find your Father!
You will find your life!
You will find Christ Jesus!
You will find your true identity!
You will find your destiny and the reason for your being here on planet earth.

Matthew 11: 28 come, to me all you that are weary and burdened, and I will give you rest. Take my yoke upon you and learn from me, for I am gentle and humble in heart, and you will find rest for your souls. For my yoke is easy and my burden is light.

There can be no real meaning to life on earth and no true satisfaction in relationships unless they are centered within the life of Christ Jesus.

Christ is our reward!

Christ is our answer!

"HE IS THE TREASURE OF THE UNIVERSE AND OUR ONLY HOPE OF GLORY."

Chapter 2

THE WORD OF THE LORD

I realize that the forward and introduction has been lengthy, but I felt that I must lay the proper foundation for this book and the reason that I believe. We all are open books to be read by men of the ways of God. This then is my story of the Mercy and Grace of Almighty God. In the following pages you will see how this God that I so fondly speak of has lead me by paths that I did not know. For I have travelled the dark path through the Valley and the following are the things that I have experienced.

For He has protected me, provided for me over a space of 58 years to bring me to the place that I stand today and whose everlasting love sustains me even now. I have gone through the Valley of Decision and paid the price to know the truth and now I have come back to encourage those of you who are about to begin their journey to know the "Truth" himself.

Many years ago early in my walk within a few months after I had given my life to Christ. I was visiting Pastor Lavern Campell's Church in Dunwoody Georgia. One Sunday morning after the service I was walking up the gravel drive to my car when I sensed that someone was behind me, I turned to look and saw no one, it was just as I turned back around that I heard a voice say the following words,
"I am going to make you an example."
Out loud with no embarrassment still walking towards my car I said, an example of what? This voice said, "**I am going to make you an example of my patience, my longsuffering and my love."**
I said, and to whom will this example be made?
Again this voice said**, "I am going to make you an example of my patience, my longsuffering and my love, to my people, and they will know that I am the Lord thy God."**
I was not aware that I just had an experience with the God who created me nor did it bring me any comfort. It would be many years before I would come to know the depth of those words, never mind the experiences that I would have to go through so that one day I could embrace them as flesh of my flesh and bone of my bone.
My personal life has been a long series of crisis's and failures in the whirlwinds of great chaos. I have spent much of my life steeped in the manic depression and self-loathing and hell-bent on self-destruction. I have attempted suicide many times over the nearly 58 years that I have walked this earth. From the ages 7 to 36 years I have spent my life in the

confines of darkness and my own self designed mental prison. But through all the events in my life and for all the crisis's in my life that I considered negative and destructive, I now look back and see the hand of a patient, long-suffering and all loving God leading me and protecting me until I could be brought to and walk through the valley of the shadow of death. So that one day, I would be able to declare to the world with all my heart, the everlasting love of this Eternal God.

And this is the reason for the writing of this book.

This was His perfect will for my life that I might identify with his sufferings and that through His sufferings, I might partake of His divine nature having been accepted as one of His many sons through Christ Jesus.

Romans 8:17 now if we are children then we are heirs-heirs of God and co-heirs with Christ Jesus, if indeed we share in his sufferings in order that we may also share in his glory.

The greatest changes in our lives will come in the midst of the greatest chaos. Our lives will be transformed and revolutionized and our natures will be changed to be like His, if we understand that every soul must walk this Valley.
And walk it alone.
Dependent on His marvelous grace to sustain us.

God uses the chaos and the crisis's that we have created through our rebellion, ignorance and arrogance in our lives as instruments to gently lead us by paths we are not familiar with for our eternal benefit. Moreover, our lives will be changed forever because of the great love this God has for us in His son Christ Jesus.

When this amazing love is shed abroad in our hearts we will be changed to be like Him. For we will have found our life in Him. And Him alone.

The pain that we carry in our soul is allowed by God so that He alone might fill it with the power of His holy presence. He desires to fill the void that He created for himself with his perfect love.

For His amazing love endures forever!

For He has crowned us with compassion!

Pain... whether we like it or not is therefore a necessary part of the process of identification with Christ Jesus to become one with him. This revelation to our spirit and soul will only be found in the Valley of God. My life was anything but normal even as a little boy I was introduced early on to the darkness of soul and negative feelings that would become my closest companions of my journey of life.

At the age of seven years old while sleeping one night I was awakened by the presence of someone in my room. I slept alone as I was the only male child in the in the family with four sisters and I was the eldest. In a room that was completely dark with the doors and windows locked from the inside. I was awakened from a sound sleep as though someone had placed their hand squarely on my shoulders.

As was the case I slept in my shorts with no shirt on and to be awakened in this way scared me nearly to death. I jumped up into the corner of my bed trembling with fear unable to see anything except the darkness. After what seemed to be hours I finally worked up the nerve to reach over and turn all the light. Immediately, I looked around the room and then rolled over and looked under the bed then ran and threw open the closet door. I jumped up on my dresser to see if anyone was hiding in the loft. When no one was found I checked the windows and doors to see if they are still locked. And they were.

I remember standing in the middle of my little bedroom wondering if what I had just experienced with real or imagined. I turned around to my mirror and I saw a pressure imprint of a hand that was larger than mine. I tried to see if I can put my hand in the same position.

Maybe I had rolled over on my own hand, but no matter how I tried I was unable to place my hand in the same position never mind the size difference. At least 10 to 15 minutes having lapsed during this event before I stood before the mirror and the pressure imprint was still visible. I tried sleep that night but I was not able to as it was more than I could comprehend. Something profound had happened to me that night, and I would never be the same.

Many years later I was praying and the Holy Spirit brought to my remembrance that night when I was so young,

And said, **you were sealed that night and were set apart for the work of God.**

Scripture Ezra 7:28 and I was strengthened as the hand of the Lord my God was upon me.

I never said anything to anyone what happened that night and in looking back I'm not sure why. The experience of that night was seared deeply into my memory. From that day forward my life began to change drastically in every way possible. My school-work began to suffer and I withdrew from relation-ships. In school I would sleep from class to class and the teachers would give me a passing grade so that I would not be held back.

I did not have any friends and all my classmates sensed there was something different about me and I was singled out. I continued to sink deeper into depression. Loneliness and darkness became my only friends.

At school I would get into fights nearly every day but I would never defend myself. I would have to run home just ahead of those wanting to harm me. At five minutes till 3 pm, I would turn my desk towards the door just to get a head start.

I didn't know why I was so disliked by those I came in contact with even those in my own family. I would run all the way home from the bus stop only to be caught at the fence gate to my house and beaten as my dad watched from the front porch drinking a beer. On one occasion he told me that I was a coward and that he had had enough of watching me get beat up, and if I did not start fighting back, each time I lost a fight he was going to beat me within an inch of my life.

I was about eight or nine when I was caught by my father engaged in a sexual act that so enraged him that he nearly beat me to death. He beat me with a leather belt for what seemed to be an eternity. He left the room only to come back and do it all over again, never saying a word as he delivered the punishment. I was bloody and bruised from my face to my feet when he had finished.

Over 30 years later I asked him in the only conversation that I had with him on that subject since that night, I asked, do you remember the beating that you gave me when I was a little boy? He said yes I do,

I said, I thought you were going to beat me to death that night.

He said, I intended too.

I lived in a family where violence was the norm. My dad was a violent alcoholic having grown up in a very violent home himself. One evening there was a family meeting at the dining room table. As I walked into the room I saw my father with his back to me and with a beer can held high, he said, I swear from this date forward I no longer have a son! At that moment in my life the very spirit of who I was drained completely out of me. In my mind on that day it was if I had never been born, my life was over. My dad said, it is obvious that you have way too much time on your hands so I will find things around here to keep you busy.

To start with I want the basement dug out so I can walk down there and light the furnace. I want deep enough to stand up in with these measurements 6x12x8 feet.

Every day after school you'll come home change clothes and dig until supper. After supper you will go and continue to dig until bedtime. There will be no football, baseball or anything else the other kids do your age. When I come home from work if there hasn't been enough dirt removed to satisfy me, I will beat you again within an inch of your life.

No one ever asked me how I had been introduced to this behavior nor did they ask me if I had been molested. No one cared. My childhood had ended and I was sentenced to death and sent into the crawlspace.

My dad took me out to the opening in the crawlspace, and I was given a light bulb on an extension cord and a short handle pick and shovel. The crawlspace was so low that I had to lay of my stomach and dig a hole deep enough to stand up in and then throw the dirt up into a 3 x 3' concrete box that I had to build.

I would then crawl up into the box and shovel the dirt into a wheelbarrow and wheel it out into the yard. For nearly eight months every day I dug what would become my own grave. The red Georgia clay was hard from the years of us children riding our tricycles over the area that had become the room addition to the rear of our house. Many nights I would lean up against the cold red clay dirt walls and cry and sink deeper into the depression and darkness. It was here that the spirits of death and suicide came up alongside me and would travel with me for many years. I now had some friends, my only friends…

Darkness, death and suicide.

My first attempt suicide was during the basement event when I took 45 aspirins. I just wanted to die, and the truth was I was already dead emotionally and psychologically. I had been rejected by my parents and by those at my school and was alone in my pain. I was alone in my darkness without any hope. I took the aspirins went back to bed, but later I arose and went back into the kitchen and drank nearly a gallon of milk. I don't know if the milk diluted aspirins that I had taken but I had no ill effects. This would be the first of many attempts to destroy myself on a journey that would be filled with deep depression, suicidal thoughts and actions, sexual perversions, and self-loathing. This would also be the first of many times that the hand of God would intervene and save me.

My life would be filled with chaos going from crisis to crisis and failure upon failure.

My school life continued to suffer as I was introduced to drugs. I thought the drugs would help me medicate the pain in my heart. One day I was turned onto black gngee and the next day I was doing orange sunshine and purple haze acid. But the drugs only made things worse by further distorting my already messed up reality. But that didn't stop me from running the gambit of drugs including LSD. My whole life continued to deteriorate and I eventually quit school after failing the 10th grade. The only bright spot in my school life was my 10th grade American History teacher by the name of Mrs. Welzant. One morning just after the bell rang I went into her classroom having just smoked some pot in the boy's restroom. As soon as I got to my desk I put my head down to sleep as was my routine. It was just then that I saw her coming over from underneath my crossed arms and she stood beside me. She took a deep breath and I knew she could smell the pot I had just smoked.

She took her hand and made a fist and began to gently hit me on the top of my head and she said the following, Randall, I know that you are in there. And I know that you are smart enough to pass my class, and pass my class you will!

At that point in my life I did not know what words of encouragement sounded like. I was so hungry for any words of encouragement that when I heard her say those words, I woke up temporarily from my self-induced coma and passed her class with the only B grade I received in high school.

I will never forget her words…

I will never forget her… She gave me a love for American history.

I was constantly getting into arguments with the family and one night it came to head. At 15 years old I got into a fight with my dad and he told me that if I was going to continue to live under his roof that I would be subject to even more of his beatings and that he would beat me every day. I said, Old Man, I have gotten use to your beatings. You can beat a dog only so long and he begins to like the pain... He told me that if that were the case that I had better leave right then and there or ***he was going to kill me.***

So on a Saturday night around 2am I took the sheet off my bed and loaded everything that I owned and made my way to the stop sign at the end of my street. I sat there for an hour or so. I could see the lights still on in the den. I knew that they were still up talking about the evening's event.

So I walked back and opened the back door stuck my head in and asked for the keys to the 65vw bug my mother had bought for me from an accident settlement. I had been doing yard work to pay it off and it was to be become mine at 16. I stuck my head in the door and asked if I could have the keys to the VW so that I could at least have a place to sleep. He jumped up and threw the keys at me and said take it the car and don't you ever come back here again. Don't bring your family or children around here either. I never want to see you again. If I do you know what will happen.

Of course, he did not use the King's English...

I took the backseat out of my VW piled all my clothes into a mattress and slept on the side of the road and in shopping center parking lots. I would bathe in service station restrooms and pick up bottles for returns to eat and buy gas. I did this for quite some time until I found a job and got a room by the week off Old Dixie Highway in Forest Park Georgia.

I worked for the Morrison Food Company 12 hours on and 12 hours off in a sub freezer loading trucks for their restaurants. I would spend the 12 hours off sleeping, nurturing my depression and all the unarticulated pain that I was carrying my heart. I did not need to use drugs to help me find the place of darkness and depression. All I had to do was close my eyes.

I don't know how my mother found me, but one day she showed up and said they had been talking about my situation and that they had come to the conclusion that I might be better off in the military.

I agreed, I said I would go in the military but not into the Army as my dad had been.

I wanted nothing to do with any identification with him at all.

I hated him just as much if not more than I hated myself.

So at 17,

I signed up to go into the United States Marine Corps.

Chapter 3

"EXTREME BOOT CAMP"

I went to Paris Island South Carolina and it was there that I received some discipline and order in my otherwise chaotic life never mind the overwhelming pain that I continued to carry in my heart. Paris Island was an environment that I was all too familiar with.

One night towards the end of my training I was ordered to pull guard duty. I was not informed of the area that I would be patrolling until I picked up my weapon from the armory. I was given a loaded M16 and told to walk a post around the base chapel.

It was here after many years that I would again have yet another experience like the one in my bedroom many years before. For several hours I walked around the Base Chapel that was empty and dark. Just before dawn as I turned the corner there before me was a presence that caused me to fall on my face weeping uncontrollably. I did not know who or what stood before me nor did I understand why I was weeping out loud as I was.

For a space of about 15 minutes I wept as if my life depended upon it. Laying there on the concrete I cried from the deepest part of my being. I wept not knowing in my natural mind what was going on and least of all what was happening to me.

Years later I would come to understand that I had had an encounter with Almighty God and the meaning of my name would one day reflect this encounter.

This would lay the foundation for many future encounters to come in my life where I would turn a corner and meet Him standing before me. Most times I was unaware that it was the Lord due to the unarticulated pain that blinded me from seeing Him in the Spirit.

I do not know how the other guards walking their posts did not hear my weeping. I regained my composure and finished my patrol around the Chapel. I finished my training and was deployed at Camp Lejeune North Carolina and later deployed at Georgia Tech as a reservist. I was never promoted from a private. I entered the Marine Corp, to finish my education and to go to college. But even here I could not get away from my failures and disappointments.

This was a dream that would never come to fruition for my reality would not allow it. The war in Southeast Asia was drawing to an end and government grants for school were very hard to come by.

When I realized that I was not going to receive the benefits that I had been promised I went **_AWOL_** and never went back. I was given a general/honorable discharge many years later.

My failures came to the forefront to walk with me along with my acute depression and self-loathing. It seemed that I could not obtain or retain the smallest of successes. I had been so emotionally and mentally fractured that I was basically a dead man walking. No matter how hard I tried, no matter how good my intentions were, I would always find myself in the throes of a crisis and eventually failure.

While living at home it was drilled into my head every day that I would never amount to anything. I was told that I was loser and a failure and my life was the convincing reality factor.

Mostly by my father who projected all his failures onto me.

Chapter 4

COMING BACK HOME AGAIN

After years of depression and darkness I now had voices in my head constantly reminding me of those words of days past. All I could hear were the words of my father being played over and over like a record player.

I was convinced... and my life reflected those words. I could not turn off the record player, and the more that I listened the more that my life mirrored what I was listening to within.

I had nothing to compare them to and so I embraced them completely not knowing that I was forming an image of myself. These words and the image were so strong that inwardly I did not have the strength to fight them. I hated my life with a passion and I did not want to live for any reason. And the voices in my head were all too eager to help me to that end.

In 1976 I met and married a young girl of 17 and she gave me 2 wonderful sons. I wanted to do right by her and love her and my sons but I could not give them what they needed and what they deserved. I did not have it within me. I was an open grave of pain and darkness. I tried my very best but I knew that the results would be what they had always had been.

When I said, I do, I dumped all my pain, unresolved issues and emotional baggage at her feet. After 7 years she said she had had enough of my violence, darkness, and failures and she filed for divorce.

During the marriage I lacked motivation and could not hold down a job. We were always in crisis with financial problems with the lights and the phone etc. The cars that we owned were constantly breaking down the rent wasn't being paid and we were always hiding from creditors.

I had brought my crisis into her life and now I had a partner to go to crisis to crisis with. Misery loves company and I had brought them both.

I was now responsible for the crisis in their lives and the self-condemnation was more than I could bear.

When the divorce was final I was so devastated that I took the Chevy Vega that I owned and slammed it into the retaining wall at 85mph on 1-285 near Jonesboro road. When the car hit the wall my head hit the driver's window and blew it out. My head then hit the concrete retaining wall knocking me unconscious. The first responders had to use the Jaws of Life to execrate me from the car.

The accident tied traffic up for over an hour and I was rushed to Clayton General Hospital where I spent one night and was released.

Again, Death had eluded me once more.

I was a failure even here.

This event only galvanized me in my anger and made me all the more determined to get off a planet that had no use for me.

I went to Mt. Paran Church of God on advice of a friend to look at their bulletin board. There I found an ad for a basement apartment in Buckhead near downtown Atlanta for $200.00 a month. The ad was placed by an 88 year old Christian widow who needed her lawn cut and help around the house. In my situation this was all that I was capable of doing.

The basement was eight feet wide and just over six feet high and sixteen feet long. It smelled of dry mold from decades past and had its share of roaches, spiders and rats. I slept on an old couch for a bed and the old lady provided an old black and white TV for my use. The kitchen was out in the open with all the pipes exposed. The toilet sat out in the middle of the floor without any walls just a few feet away from the kitchen sink. The room was damp and dark and I soon realized that I was back at home. All the chaos and all the crisis in my life had brought me full circle and I now found myself back where I started...

Back at home...back where I belonged...
in the basement.

Shortly after I moved in I decided to frame the toilet area with a few 2x4's and some sheetrock. I did not finish the inside with sheetrock and it was open. I went in one evening and sat down only to look over and see a small garter snake coiled up on top of the toilet paper. I just sat there and hung my head down and thought how much lower can my life sink? I spent months doing very little and existing on the barest of means. Raking yards and picking up trash anything that the community would offer. I did have brief moments where I could hold a job for a few weeks of even several months but they were short lived and I would soon come to crisis again and it would go to failure. These moments were nothing more than futile attempts to try and fix my life. During this time the only thing that would leave me with a feeling that I was still human was masturbation. This was chronic in my behavior but I felt that I needed at least one vice that made me feel alive. Even this was a pathetic attempt to self-medicate and escape my pain. My depression was now manic and I was not aware just how unmanageable it had become. I was nearly incapacitated and yet somehow I worked up enough nerve to try and work things out with my ex-wife. Again...

I even gave my life to the Lord during this time, as I would have done anything to have her back in my life. I wanted to prove to her that I could change and hoped that this decision for the Lord would sway her to give me one more chance. I had given my life to the Lord for all the wrong reasons. I was baptized with my family in the audience and believed with all my heart that this would win her back. I gave her a new engagement ring and I thought that we were on the road to reconciliation, but she got cold feet at the last second and rejected my offer and me. Looking back I now know that I had used Christ for my agenda. This error would cost me many future disappointments until my mindset could be changed. With her rejection of my reconciliation my chaos peaked into another crisis, and I decided to try and kill myself yet one more time.

It is important here to note that my attempts to take my life were not cries for help, but they were my futile attempts to escape the pain of a broken heart and the decades of failures. Moreover, the unrelenting voices in my head that constantly told me that I was a loser and would never amount to anything.

The voices in my head were now speaking clearly the only internal language that I understood. I gave in once again and agreed that I should go ahead and kill myself doing everyone a favor. I took the van that I had just bought up to the Baptist Church on the corner of Peachtree Street and Wieuca Road. I locked the keys inside and walked to the drug store and bought 4 packages of the strongest sleeping tablets and went back to the apartment. When I got back I called the finance company and told them to come and get the van that I no longer wanted it. I took all my clothes, fishing equipment and emptied out the unit.

Chapter 5

FROM THE GRAVE

The only things left inside were the furnishings that came when I moved in. The last thing I did was to stand at the trash can behind my unit, where in anger and outrage I swore at God tearing to pieces the Thompson Chain International Bible that a friend had given me only a few months earlier. I swore at the Lord at the top of my voice tearing my bible into a 1000 pieces and with my fist raised to the heavens I railed at him screaming,

"This thing called Christianity ain't working for me!"

I went back into the apartment and sat down and opened all four packages of the sleeping tablets piling them up on the end table. I got a large glass of water and with one hand full after another I began to swallow all 48 tablets. Once I had swallowed all the pills I sat down in the rocking chair and began to speak out loud.

And this is what I shouted... "I don't know why my life has been a series of failures. I don't know why I was born or why I have experienced all this pain. I don't know why I go from crisis to crisis and I don't know what awaits me on the other side, but it has to be a damned sight better than what I have experienced here.

And even if it ain't, I do not care! I no longer care one way or the other! No matter what, I am going to die tonight, and nothing and no one will stop me! I am finished with living on this planet!
Tonight I will die!
I will go to sleep and the next thing I will know is nothing!

It was just then that I heard a gentle voice speak as though someone was there in my room with me.

This gentle voice said, ***'It will not work my son, for I have called you."***

This only infuriated me and I screamed back at the voice, watch me!

I am going to die tonight!

And once again the words came, '' It will not work my son, for I have called you."

I sat back in the rocking chair and waited for what I believed would certain death and that right soon. I waited for hours for the sleeping pills take affect and to fall into deep sleep and death.

And never once did I even nod off.

I stood up at sunrise and with my fists clinched I continued to rail at the voice that had spoken to me in the night. With all the anger and pain that I could muster in my heart, I screamed and cursed at the voice who had intervened and canceled my plan to destroy myself.

I told Him that he had no right to keep me alive against my will!
And I told Him that I hated Him!

A few days later I called the wife of one the guys that I had worked with installing contract cable TV. He had married a Christian woman and they were attending a small church over in Gwinnett County. I told her that I was having some serious problems but I did not go into detail. Joyce asked me if she sent her husband Rory to pick me up would I go to their church one evening. At this point in my life I felt that things could not get any worse or so I thought. So I said yes…

And the next evening I walked through the doors of Christ fellowship of Atlanta. The church was very small and services were being held in a renovated warehouse. It was there that Wednesday evening that I would meet the first spiritual man that would speak directly into my heart. A man who would forever change my life by speaking words of love and wisdom from the very heart of God, and my destiny and my eternal reward would be set that night.

His name is Pastor Chuck Strong.

There were only about 20 people in attendance on that Wednesday evening and I found a seat near the doors so I could leave at a moment's call. I had only gone to church a couple of times in my life and I did not know what to expect.

Around 7pm a thin wispy sort or man entered the sanctuary and put his bible on the pulpit. Within a couple of minutes he turned to me and said, brother do I know you? Looking down at the floor I nodded in the negative. Again he asked, have you ever been here before?

Again, I nodded in the negative.

He said, come up here, the Spirit of the Lord wants to minister to you this evening.

I moved up front and stood before him as he put his hands on my forehead and began to pray. And once again I began to weep with the same intensity that I had that night when I pulled guard duty in boot camp. The more he prayed the more I wept until I felt as though I would collapse. After a few minutes things quieted down and Pastor Chuck began to speak in a gentle voice over me.

He said, brother, I am going to tell you what I see in the Spirit and the words that I hear in the Spirit. It was the Spirit of the Lord that brought you here this evening.

There has been a conspiracy from the pits of hell to take your life from early on. But I am here tonight to tell you that the plan of the enemy to destroy your soul will not succeed. For you are called of God.

Let me tell you the words that I hear in the spirit. All those people that said that you would never amount to anything, that you were worthless, the day is coming and I hear this in the Spirit, when they will stand in amazement as to the great works God has done in you and through you. And they will surely say they are amazed at the changes that have taken place in your life. Yes, they will say that the changes they see are surely of God and give Him glory, honor and praise.

Every negative word that was ever uttered against you will be silenced and you shall glorify God. For you are called of God.

The man saying these words to me did not know the words that I had screamed out to God several nights earlier. Nor did he know about the pain in my heart.

For I had told no one.

Once again I was standing at a corner in my life with this presence in front of me touching the deepest part of my being.

And all I could do was stand there and weep from the deepest part of my soul.

There behind Pastor Chuck was a man name Randy Webb and Pastor Chuck turned to him and said, Randy, come and put your arms around this man for Almighty God is redeeming him from the very grave tonight.

Redeeming me from the very grave.

All my life I had lived with a perfect hatred for my life and with a passion for death. I lived my life as one dead man, a walking corpse. But now that cold, hard and dry broken heart was receiving the healing waters of life. The very voice that I had screamed and railed at, was now pouring His perfect love over into my heart.

My heart was being healed.

It was as though God himself was holding my broken heart in his hands. Deep had cried out to the deep and the deep had answered.

And the deep waters of Almighty God were crashing over me in wave after wave.

He was making me free... He was healing my heart...

He was making me His son...

I was coming out of my grave!

The grave that I had dug when I was a little boy!

I was being born again!

The door to my heart was beginning to open, yet it would be many more years before I would truly understand the full ramifications of that Wednesday night. Never mind the experiences that still lay ahead of me and the level of trust and faith that would be required of me if I were to arrive at my destiny in God through Christ Jesus.

I began to get involved with the church and I would go as often as I could afford it. The only car I had at the time was on old Toyota Corolla that someone had given me. The car had been driven up from South America and it had bullet holes in the rear quarter panel where it had been shot at by the Sandinistas. It was junk and had no tag or insurance and the windows and heater did not work. I was still as dysfunctional as I was before I arrived at Christ Fellowship unable to maintain and move forward.

But I felt that maybe I was on track.

One Sunday morning Pastor Chuck preached a message on how the Lord wants to be involved in every area of our lives. Even the simplest of things like fishing. Little did I know how deeply this sermon would affect me forever and not too many days down the road?

During the preaching Pastor Chuck would come to a scripture that he wanted to emphasize and drive home.

He spoke about John 8:32 "If you hold to my teaching, you are really my disciples. Then you will know the truth, and the truth will make you free."

When Pastor Chuck came to the word in the scripture and the truth will what? Well, I knew that scripture so I jumped to my feet and shouted, He will set you free!

Thinking that I had answered correctly I sat down only to hear from the pulpit the words, **_"He will make you free."_**

Once again Pastor Chuck read the same scripture and again at the word "Then, you will know the truth and the truth will what?

I jumped up yet again and shouted, He will set you free!

I sat down and again from the pulpit I heard, ***He will make you free.***

Pastor Chuck did this three times and after the 3rd time I became somewhat angry because I felt he was calling me out to look foolish and before the church. After all, I had my bible with me and it said ***"set."***

It would be many years before I would realize that there is a great difference between **being made free** and **being set free.** This would be one of the hardest lesson that I would embrace on my journey.

John 8:32 alone would become most important to me and come to play a very significant role in my life, and the way that I would perceive and come to understand the ways of God in dealing with me.

Chapter 6

GONE FISHIN

A s it had been for several years before I arrived Christ Fellowship would go to the mountains for a spiritual retreat over the Labor Day weekend. I had been working with Rory Knapton and his Christian band doing whatever was needed basically just a gofer. His wife Joyce asked me if I would consider going with the church and helping out with the band. I told her that I would go but I did not want to be involved in the meetings. I was going because I had heard that there was a 45 acre lake and I wanted to fish it. I did not know that she had given up her hotel room so that I could go. I said that I would drive the truck with all the equipment and unload it when I arrived. So early on Friday afternoon I left for Lake June Aluska, North Carolina, driving a loaded Ryder rental truck. When I arrived it was getting late into the afternoon and it took me about 3 hours to unload the truck and set everything in place in the Chapel.

When I had finished I walked out onto the balcony that overlooked the 45 acre lake. The sun was about to set and the lake surface was like glass. It was just then that the sermon that Pastor Chuck preached a few weeks before came to my mind. You know the one about God that he desires to get involved even the simplest things even fishing.

So right there on the balcony I said out loud, Lord, you know how much I love to fish, but I know that I could go down there and beat those banks to death and not catch anything.

My mindset of failures even affected my prayers.

My conversation continued, Even so, I believe that you know where the fish are and I am asking that you tell me where to go.

Not expecting to hear anything what so ever, I gathered my equipment and went to the water's edge. Just as I set my rod and reel down I heard that gentle voice that I had heard before in my basement apartment. And He said, *"Stand between this pillar and that post."*

I looked and the space between the pillar and the post was about 50 feet. I looked in my tackle box and saw a lot of lures and not knowing which one to use I again asked, Lord which one do I use?

I did not hear his voice respond this time but I felt that I should use one of my top water lures. I threw out the plug and as soon as it hit the water I had my first largemouth bass. She came up out of the water and danced on top. Within a few minutes I had caught and landed 6 bass and all of them having danced on the water on their tails. They weighed between 2lbs and the largest was nearly 3lbs.

Pastor Chuck pulled up on the grass near where I was fishing and opened the door and asked was I having any luck?

I told him that I had caught several bass in just a few minutes and that I was having a blast. The next morning before breakfast I went back to the same spot and picked up where I had left off the evening before. This time the fish were even larger and the top water action even more spectacular. My total was now 13 and they were pushing 4 and half pounds.

All this was taking place while the church was having their meetings and classes in the hotel. Somehow the word got around that I was catching fish and people started showing up to watch me fish.

I found myself giving fishing classes' right there between the pillar and the post. And everyone who followed my instructions and stood where I had stood caught their first bass and they danced on the water just like mine had done. The hotel's balcony overlooked the lake and after breakfast many of the people would sit and watch me fish. When I caught one, I could hear them exclaim, He's got another one! Look at that one dance!

This happened all day long even late into the evening and before I was finished that day, I had more fish than I had ever caught in my life! Even bigger fish and better quality fish and they all had danced on the water.

I had caught all these fish in one spot with one lure and I had had the best time in my life! I was elated to say the least.

That night I had trouble sleeping as I rehearsed over in my mind what I had experienced in the past few hours. I could not sleep so I went down to the chapel as I still had the key. I unlocked the door and locked it behind me and went down to the Altar.

There above me was one light and it shone on me as I knelt before God and began to pray... Not having been a praying man I opened my mouth and began to talk out loud to the Lord just as I had done on the balcony. As soon as I opened my mouth I was overcome with a feeling that I had never known before. I was well acquainted with negative feelings, negative feelings had been my only friends. This feeling was altogether new and refreshing and alive.

I was overcome with gratitude and thanksgiving.

It was the presence of God just like I had experienced walking guard duty in boot camp.

I spent quite some time there on the floor weeping in gratitude and thanksgiving. With my tears falling on the floor I said, Lord, I know that you heard my prayer and you answered. I have had the best time that I have ever had fishing in my entire life. I am so very thankful for all that you have done for me. But most of all for hearing my prayer.

I said, Lord I can only think of one thing that would top this weekend off, and that would be to catch a bass just a little bigger than the biggest one that I have ever caught.

With that I went to room and tried to sleep but the feelings of gratitude and thanksgiving continued to flood my being. I felt alive for the first time in my life and I knew it was God.

I arose and went to the same spot only this morning it was overcast and raining albeit softly. I made several casts and only caught one small one and he was the smallest of the weekend. Steve Perigin was sitting up on the balcony and hollered down to me that if I wanted to eat breakfast I had better hurry as the cafeteria was closing.

I looked up to the clouds and said out loud, Lord this is my last cast!

And with those words I launched my lure out into the deepest part of the lake. When my lure hit the water the water exploded! It looked and sounded as if someone had dropped a concrete block from a helicopter. And I knew that I had a huge bass on my line. Moreover, I knew that God had heard and answered my prayer, and I had the biggest bass of my life on the other end. Knowing from experience that when a bass is hooked she will run to cover and try to tear the hook out of her mouth and or break the line. There is a certain amount of fear you have that you might lose the fish during the fight.

After all, she is fighting for her life.

But the feelings of failure and loss that I had experienced so many times before in my life were not there. As I stood there holding onto the biggest fish of my life, I began to be showered with wave after wave of a feeling and awareness that I would come to understand as the Love of God.

I stood there in perfect peace for the first time in my life while the biggest bass of my life was on the other end. My rod was doubled and she was trying to pull me into the lake. I stood there and wept as I had wept at the altar only a few hours before.

And just like before I heard a gentle voice speak to me, and He said,

"*I have called you to fish for the souls of men. You will not have to strive for them, for I will bring them to you.*"

The voice that I heard that day was gentle and filled with love. And I knew that I had heard the voice of Almighty God.

And the tears that I cried that day were tears of joy.

My dad had never spent time with me and never had taken me fishing. Yet, there on this Sunday morning I found myself fishing with the God of all Creation. I fought her for what seemed to be an hour but in reality it was only a few minutes. I did however lose my grip on time during this experience. I finally got control of her and reached down and pulled her up on the bank and laid her in the grass. A light rain began to fall as I put my rod and reel down and stood back in amazement. There before me was the biggest bass of my life and she weighed 9lbs and 9and1/2 oz. My previous best was 7lbs and

¾ oz. and I had not mentioned this in my prayer at the altar.

I was so happy that I danced up and down that little foot path before the Lord. Singing Praises and shouting to Him telling Him how grateful and thankful I was to Him. I had never danced before in my life for any reason and there I was dancing up and down that foot path in the rain with my arms raised praising my God for all that He had done for me. That little boy who was walking in a man's body, who had been carrying so much unarticulated pain, and who had been forced to dig his own grave; who lived in a world of darkness and depression for decades; that same little boy who had experienced more negative feelings than good feelings, was now dancing and shouting for joy in the presence of His God. I had gone to the mountains for my own selfish reasons and once again I had turned the corner and found myself standing in the presence of God Almighty. I had gone to be alone only to find myself alone with my God.

And once more, He was holding my heart in his mighty hands.

1 Peter 2:9-10
You are of a chosen generation, a royal priesthood, a holy, holy nation, a special people belonging to God, that you should show forth the praises of Him who has called you out of darkness into his marvelous light.

Psalms 116-1-2
I love the Lord, because He has heard my
voice and my supplications, because He
has inclined His ear to me, therefore, I will
call on Him as long as I live.
I was being made free from within.
I was being made free one step at a time
on His path unto His righteousness.
I was beginning to understand.
I was coming out of the darkness and I
was singing His praises.
I was coming out of my darkness into His
marvelous light.
I was dancing in His marvelous light.
Giving thanks to Him who has delivered
me from the power of darkness.
Praise the Lord, O my soul, praise
the Lord!

I loaded my fish into the rental truck and went and bought a cooler and some ice. She was so big that she hung out of both ends of the cooler. When I arrived back at the hotel I went to the cafeteria to find Pastor Chuck still eating breakfast. I told him that I really needed to see him and that I had something very important to show him in my room. It took some convincing but he finally agreed and we went to my room.

When we arrived I showed him the answer to my prayers and he could do nothing but stand there in amazement and declared, "this is a sign from God!

He asked me to bring her to the chapel and show her to the congregation.

It was truly a Sunday morning to be remembered.

And many of God's people were encouraged on that day.

On Monday, I went to check out and as I was standing there the manager of the hotel asked, are the one everyone is talking about? I said, it depends on what they are saying. She responded and asked me if I was the individual that had caught all the fish?

I said, I am. She said, well we find that very difficult to believe. I said, how so? She said, we had a chemical/ sewage spill in the creek north of here and it polluted the entire lake. The spill was so severe that we had a complete fish kill. The EPA came in and told us that the lake was basically dead and if there were any fish left not to eat any of them.

So, we find it very hard to believe that you caught any fish at all in that lake.

I said, well I did.

With her statement, that made my weekend there all the more miraculous. I pulled the truck up along the shoulder of the lake with my fish on ice, I sat there gazing out over the picturesque view drinking in the beauty of a place that had forever changed my heart. I turned and started for home with my heart full of gratitude and thanksgiving for a weekend that I would never forget. I began to weep out of joy and contentment for my desire to fish had been satisfied, but moreover I now knew that the Creator of the Universe would incline his ear to my voice and my prayer. I had gone to the mountains to fish by myself and ended up fishing with the God who created the mountains and the lakes. I had tasted His tender mercies and been bathed in His peace that surpasses all understanding. I had tasted His amazing love that endures forever. And that same amazing love had been poured over into my heart. I would never be the same... Even this evening as I rewrite these words my heart breaks with knowing this reality.

Chapter 7

STILL MAKING MISTAKES

A gentle rain began to fall as I started my long drive home, as I began to recount the events my heart swelled with tears of thanksgiving. I wept all the way to Atlanta pouring my heart out to the One that had touched me so deeply, at times I could not see the road for my tears.

I was being healed. I was being restored to wholeness. The God of Love had captured my heart. I was becoming a human being. I was being made into a son.

> **_Our God is an Awesome God! He reigns from heaven from above!_**
> **_With Wisdom and power and Love! Our God is an Awesome God!_**

After reading all the above one might think that after having several intimate experiences with the presence of the Lord that that same person would get his life on track and that it would be the end of the story. But, in my case nothing could be further from the truth. For you see, in being made free one must face by faith the demons that sought to destroy him and rob him of his destiny. He must become an overcomer by faith to the glory and praise of God. And in doing so he becomes part of the Army of God. This requires trust, submission, faith and a lifestyle of humility and brokenness. The hard ground of my heart had been broken open by the living waters of God, and now the cornerstone could be laid in my heart. Many more dark experiences awaited me and my passage through them would increase my faith and my trust in God. All along my path the God who had been with me that weekend would continue to reveal himself to me in the inner most places. A tried and sure foundation must be laid deep within our hearts and this requires a deep purging.

This purging can only be done by the Holy Spirit. Our pride and arrogance keeps Him at bay and keeps us in great darkness and delays our spiritual development. The spirits of rejection, fear, self-loathing, murder, lust and suicide that sought to destroy my soul and rob me of my destiny in Christ, were now being exposed in the light of God that was now shining into my heart. My spiritual eyes were just beginning to open slowly even as a new born eyes open after birth. I was being born again…

John 3:7 You should not be surprised at my saying. You must be born again.

I remember coming home to my apartment one night and just as I got to the door I heard the voice that I had heard many times before and He said, "It will be the 2nd key that you could to." I carried a set of keys that numbered over 30 and many of them looked alike. Standing at the door at 1am with very little light I would fumble for the right one every night. This experience happened several times over a period of a week and always at the door. I ignored the voice every time even though I had had all those previous experiences before. I just could not believe that God would speak to me on such a small matter. So one night as I arrived at my door I said out loud, Ok Lord, I cannot believe that you would speak to me on such an unimportant matter as to which key will unlock my door. I stood there waiting for some time and then a gentle voice spoke and said, it will be the 3rd key that you come to. I tried it and it worked.

I did this several more nights in a row going through the same routine and asking which key to use. Then one night upon opening the door I heard His gentle voice say, ***"I hold the keys to the Kingdom of God and I give them to you this night."***

The Holy Spirit holds the keys to the doors that will unlock the power of God and bring us into the riches stored up for us in Christ Jesus. When we walk in humility and brokenness before Him, the blessings of God will flow unto us just as a mighty river flows. We must be willing to listen and interact when we hear that gentle voice speaking to us.

For flesh and blood cannot inherit the Kingdom of God but only those who have been born of the spirit and of water. One of the most important things with God is that all who seek him must come before Him in humility, brokenness and a contrite spirit.

The pride of our flesh cannot stand in His Holy sanctuary. When we come in we must come in pouring out the offering that is acceptable in His sight. And He is pleased to accept us as his sons and daughters. As sons and daughters of the Most High God.

And He is pleased with our sacrifice because we have given unto Him the respect and admiration that belongs to him.

And He will lift us up in His Presence.

Humble yourself under the mighty hand of God and He will lift you up in due season.

" To the degree that you have descended into the Valley of the shadow of Death, so shall you ascend to the highest snow covered mountain peaks and declare the Glories of God. You shall give Him glory, Honour and Praise and you shall dance before Him just as I have.

But this reality will not come without its trials and testing's so that your heart might be established upon the cornerstone of truth, the rock of your salvation, which is Christ Jesus.

Chapter 8

SEVENTH INNING STRETCH

In the late 80's I started a company and was
blessed with many contracts to build offices and
do remodeling for many of the people of Christ
Fellowship Church as we were growing by leaps
and bounds. I was well onto rebuilding my life or so
I thought when one of my demons made an appear-
ance and threw my life into chaos once again. This
had always been a pattern in my life for just as I was
about to breakthrough I had a breakdown. Thinking
that things were sure in my life I tried once again
to reconcile with my wife. Early one morning I went
by her house as she lived next door to her parents.
I wanted to pay my child support and to see my
sons. She answered the door wearing the birthday
present I had bought for her a few days before. On
the couch I saw a man that I did not know getting
dress nor did I know that they had just been married
the night before and she was on her honey moon.
I looked with amazement at her and said, you are

doing exactly opposite of what you were brought up not to do. And with that I turned and kicked the screen door of the hinges into the front yard and walked to my car. As I drove down the street I heard a voice that was all too familiar who had walked with me for years.

And he said, you might as well go back and finish the job. There is nothing left for you now!

This was not the voice of the Lord. But the spirit of murder. I said out loud, you are right! There is nothing left in my life! I have lost everything! My Wife! My family! My children! So I turned the car around and went back to the house. Not being a small man at 6.0 225lbs I jumped out of the car and ran up the steps and kicked in the front door and went in after the man I had seen. He was already up and running when I came through the door.

He ran through the kitchen and tore the back door open going out onto the back porch and leaped over the rail. I was right behind him closing in fast as he raced through the carport towards the front yard. As we came into the front yard I was reaching for the tag on his shirt and it was just then that I tripped over something and I went face down in the dirt. I went down to the ground like an eagle coming in for a landing. By the time I got back up I could only stand there and watch as he was running down the street still trying to get his clothes on. I was so angry that morning that had I gotten ahold of him I would have beat him to death and then I would probably have gone in after her and killed her also. The spirit of murder and rage was alive and well in my heart. Looking back on that fateful morning I can only surmise that God had intervened in my life yet again. For when I looked around to see what could have caused me to stumble I could not find anything at all in that area and path.

The spirit of murder and rage that I had carried for decades had been reawakened. The spirits that had been imparted to me when I was child when my dad tried to beat me to death now had manifested themselves. I now had to face them head-on if I ever intended to mature spiritually and walk as a free man.

A few days later I was arrested and thrown into the Dekalb County Jail for failure to pay child support. For you see, while we were still married I had helped my wife at the time to get a job with the Dekalb County Police Department. I had been charged with contempt of court for failing to pay court ordered child support. And I would be there without bond or due process for the next 89 days.

I guess I should have been thankful that the charges weren't more serious given what I had done only a few days earlier. Upon arrival at the jail I decided to fast, pray and seek the Lord. At that time the jail was sorely overcrowded to the point that I had to sleep on the floor on a mat. Three times a day the jailer would come and unlock the door to take everyone to eat. I would stay behind. About 100 men would file out and leave and when they returned they would find me sitting in the floor reading my bible. This went on for 10 days and soon some of them came up to me and asked why didn't I go to eat with them and wasn't I hungry. I told them that I was fasting and praying to the Lord seeking answers to why my life was so messed up. Many of them walked away shaking their heads saying that I was just plain crazy.

One night as I was sleeping and an inmate woke me and said that he needed to tell me something. He said that he had over-heard some of the brothers down front say that they were going to beat me up and take all my things and that he thought I should know so I could be prepared. He continued to say that as this plan was being discussed that 2 other brothers standing nearby spoke up and said, you will not harm that man for he has done nothing to you. Since he has come in here he has done nothing but seek his God, read his bible and pray. You will not touch him or his things.

Those that wanted to harm you said, who are you his guardian angels?

They responded, call us what you will, but you will not harm him!

The inmate that told me these things patted me on the back and left.

I went back to sleep.

Chapter 9

THE PRISON WALLS WERE SHAKEN

I would have never known that this conversation had taken place had it not been for that inmate. Later he would become the first of many that I would lead to the Lord. I had been there about a month and according to seniority and time spent I was allowed to move into one of 14 pods that gave me some privacy and a bed to myself. One night while I was sound asleep I was awakened by someone knocking on my door. I arose and let him in and he introduced himself and we sat down on the edge of my bunk. He said I know that you are a man of God and I want to know the God that you know. I want to get my life on the right track. We sat there on the edge of my bunk for several hours as I shared the things and the ways of God to him. Then we got down on our knees and I led him to Christ Jesus. After my prayer we stood up and I welcomed him into the family of God. As soon as this man had given his life to the Lord someone else knocked on my door and asked if he could talk to me about my God.

I said yes come in… Before the night was over several men from outside my pod had come to pray with me. The first man went outside and sat down at my door and would announce visitors that wanted to speak to me. He did this on his own for I did not ask him. He was the first of 12 men that would give their lives to the Lord in my pod.

Some nights I would stay awake all night as one man after another would knock on my door. One night the Lord sent me a Jehovah's Witness who wanted to know the reality of God as I had ministered. He said his parents were devout but he felt that something was missing. But he knew that there was something very different about me.

And he wanted what I had.

He explained to me the teachings that he had received and I showed him in the bible where the errors lay that had brought about his desire to know the Person of the truth.

After several hours he renounced that doctrine and we got on our knees and he asked me to prayer for him that he had never really known Christ Jesus. So I prayed and he asked Jesus Christ afresh into his heart.

I would have bible study in the back of the jail 2 to 3 times a day and many of the inmates would come and participate. I knew that I needed to have a baptism for the 12 men the Lord had given me. So I had them meet me up front near where everyone watched the TV. The showers were close by, so I turned a large trash can over and stood on it over-looking the shower area. I had all 12 men enter the showers in their boxer shorts and stand under the shower heads. With the water running I had them repeat the prayer that I spoke over them. In front of 90 other inmates I baptized them in the Holy Name of the Father, Son and the Holy Spirit. When they came out I embraced each of them and welcomed them into the family of God.

While I was standing on that trash can baptizing those men, the words that I had heard in the mountains when I caught my biggest fish came rushing back into soul.

I have called you to fish for the souls of men. You will not strive for them for I will bring them to you.

And He had brought them to me.

For His Glory and Honour and Praise.

It was happening just as He had told me in the mountains. Once again I was fishing and this time I was fishing for souls and catching lots of them. The last 2 men that I would lead to the Lord before my time was through at the jail were the two men that spoke up in my defense the night the others wanted to harm me.

They were by far the meanest looking of those in our cell block as they had been convicted of drug smuggling and murder. One had killed a State Patrol officer many years before and was now in jail again awaiting trial on multiple felony charges. The very men that God had used to protect me, and the meanest men on the block had both come into my pod and gotten down on their knees and asked Christ Jesus into their lives respectively. My ministry had begun in earnest and yet I felt that I was still in great need of restoration myself. In my mind I was not whole and yet God was using me to bring others to himself.

One Sunday morning a minster from a local church came to speak and all those that wanted to go were released to go to the chapel under guard. After having listened to him and his message and having watched how his words seem to fall on deaf ears. I noticed that few if any had paid any attention and had used this outing for nothing more than a bull secession. The message was dry as toast and lacked the unction of the Holy Spirit. I was young in the Lord but I knew when a message had the power of God firing through it having sat under many of Pastor Chuck's preaching.

Before the minister left he asked if there was anyone who wanted to stand up and speak. I assumed this was an altar call so I stood up and said, I do...

He said, go ahead. As I began to speak I noticed that all of the men there that morning numbering around 70 to 80 became very quiet and gave their attention to me and to the words that I was saying. I preached on the love of God through Christ Jesus and His redeeming blood. I spoke on the Cross of

Christ and the Salvation of God through His Holy Son Christ Jesus. I spoke for only a few minutes and when I was finished I asked if there were any men in that room that wanted to know the God that I knew and be saved in the name of Jesus Christ.

Over 60 men came forward at one time to receive Christ Jesus as their Lord and Savior. The minister came up to me before I left and told me that he had been coming there for years and never had he seen such an outpouring of repentance and salvation of souls.

I said, all I did was tell them about my experiences with God and His dealings with me. This statement would become the foundation of my ministry unto God's people. For by speaking to them about how He has loved me, provided for me and protected me, that through my testimony that He might have access to their hearts as never before.

I remember the words spoken to me all those years ago,

" I going to make you an example."
"I going to make an example of my patience, my longsuffering, and my love, to my people, and they will know that I am the Lord thy God."

I can only speak about my relationship with my heavenly Father and the wonderful and mighty things that He has for me through Christ Jesus my Lord.

I give to Him who sits on high all the Glory, Honour and Praise for showing me His path unto His Righteousness and for making me one of His many sons. I will use all my experiences with Him to drive the Gospel of Jesus Christ home with His everlasting love, grace and mercy.

For the Gospel of Jesus Christ in the old English language means:

The Good,

The Glad,

The Merry News, that causes a man to leap and to dance for joy.

And the Lord gave power that day to the words that I spoke and many were saved.

And once again I danced before my God and my King with thanksgiving and gratitude.

After 89 days in jail the Lord put it on the heart of a friend of mine and she paid the $2800.00 contempt of court fine and I was released. By the time I returned all the contracts I had before going to jail had been assumed by others and I was broke again. I had to start over financially from scratch as this was a constant pattern in my life. With time on my hands I went to visit some friends of mine that also had gone to Calvary Chapel Lavern Campbell's {the first church that I attended} several years before. Tom Holmes and his wife Robin had a ministry down on the corner of Peachtree Street near Charles Stanley's Church. The ministry called Safe House ministered to the street people of Atlanta.

Chapter 10

THE RAIN

Tom and his wife would go down on Friday and
Saturday nights and play worship music to
those that had an ear. One night Tom asked me
if I would like to go and help him by setting up his
equipment etc. I said that I would and we prayed
before we left that the Lord would bless our time
and send us people to minister to for His glory. We
prayed all the way down there and even as we set up
the sound system we prayed in agreement that our
prayers would be answered. All night long bikers,
prostitutes and the homeless wandered in and out
and paid little if any attention to Tom's music. After
several hours Tom told me that he was discouraged
and wanted to pack up and leave. I told him that no
matter was their reaction was that he should continue to play as if he was just playing for Jesus himself. I set a single chair in front of him and said play
your heart out to Him.

And he did.

For after all it is all about "Jesus."

Around midnight we decided to call it a night and I started rolling up the sound cords. As I sat there I noticed a couple in the back praying over a man that they had literally dragged in off Peachtree Street. He was under the influence of drugs and alcohol to the point that he was nearly incapacitated. He was so wasted that it was all he could do to sit up in the chair straight.

The front of his shirt was soaking wet from where he had drooled for hours. I stopped wrapping cords and as I watched him and acessed his condition I said in my heart to the Lord, "Lord, I know that I am messed up and need you badly, but that man needs you more than I do."

Then I heard the voice that I had heard many times before say, ***"Go back there and tell him that I love him."***

So, I stood up and walked back gently pushing my way through the small crowd that had gathered around him. I stood before him and gently spoke the words that I had been instructed to say.

I said, ***"The Lord loves you!"*** Immediately, when I spoke those words I could see into the spirit and I saw the walls that this man had built around his heart. And when I spoke those words, I could see them hit that wall with power and I saw the wall begin to buckle and crack. And the first level of blocks began to fall.

Then The Lord said*, Tell him again!* So for the second time I said, *"The Lord loves you!*

Then the Lord said, *Tell him a third time!*

So again, even bolder I said, *The Lord loves you!*

And with those words I saw the walls in his heart completely collapse. The man who only a few minutes before could not even hold himself in a chair now stood up with his arms outstretched towards the heavens and with tears streaming down his face was praying in an unknown tongue, and praising God at the top of his lungs.

Now as this was unfolding, I noticed a group of people standing around and praying over a homosexual man that had come into the building only a few feet away. Then I heard the voice of the Lord yet again,

Do you see that man over there? I said yes, "*He said, go to him and tell him that I love Him."*

I did as I was instructed. And when I spoke those words he fell to his knees and began pouring his heart in repentance before God asking God to forgive him and cleanse him that he might receive Christ Jesus into his life. I turned around to see the first man still praising God and tears flooding down his face while all those around him stood in amazement. Now, all those people that had wandered in and out all night long now filled the place and there was no room even to stand. There were people outside looking through the windows watching these men. In looking back I am not so sure that this event did not cause traffic problems that evening as the number of people that witnessed it.

Once again I knew that God had heard our prayers and had answered them with power. Even though it was well into the midnight hour, Jesus had come to honour his word. After about 20 minutes the first man sat down and began to speak. He said that he had worked as a camera man for a Christian Television Network and that he had been passed over for a promotion several times.

He had become angry with management and he left the company and wound up leaving his family and falling into a life of drugs and alcohol abuse. He sank into a deep depression and began the long slide into self- abasement. We ministered to him for a couple of hours and before we left I went and found him a bible and wrote something encouraging in the first page for him personally. To this day I don't remember what I wrote. As we were leaving around 2am that night Tom and I saw him walking up Peachtree Street reading the words that I had written in his bible. He was reading so intently that he was not watching where he was walking. I told Tom to holler at him and tell him to be careful as he walked.

He looked up from reading his bible and the words that I had written and yelled back at us and said, that tonight Jesus had healed his broken heart and he was no longer high on drugs or alcohol. We praised God and drove out of the city. The Lord was using this vessel and I wasn't even whole in my own mind much less my soul. I was still fractured and needed the touch of the Lord myself. That night I learned that the Lord desires to extend his loving kindness and tender mercies to those around us who are less fortunate regardless of our present spiritual condition.

For I desire mercy not sacrifice. Mercy triumphs over judgment.

I was extending something so very valuable to others that I was not even aware that it existed in me before that evening.

I had extended the amazing love, compassion and mercy of the Lord to his people by being willing to act on what I had heard in the spirit by faith.

And the Lord, had answered.

Later a man who introduced himself to me as the head of the Safe House Ministry came to me and said that in all his years of ministry on the streets he had never seen such a demonstration of the work of the Holy Spirit with the power of God to heal and to deliver.

That night was a night that deeply touched the hearts of all that came to minister as much as those that had been ministered to. And more importantly my heart had been touched again by the hand of God.

In looking back I believe that setting that single chair out for Tom to sing those songs unto the Lord Jesus and to him alone was the key. I believe it brought down the glory of God upon that building that night.

I will glorify the King of kings!
I will glorify the Lamb!
I will glorify the Lord of lords for he is the Great I AM!
Lord Jehovah reigns in majesty!
I will bow before His Throne!
I will worship Him in righteousness!
I will worship him alone!
I will praise Him all the days of my life!

> ***Psalms 103:1-4 Praise the Lord, O my soul, all my being praise his holy name. Praise the Lord, O my soul, and forget not all his benefits who forgives all your sins and heals all your diseases, who redeems your life from the pit and crowns you with love and compassion, who satisfies your desires with good things so that your youth is renewed like the eagles.***

O Lord, hear the cry of my heart to follow you all the days of my life.
O Lord, hear the cry of my heart to know you as you are and to be close to you.
O Lord, open my eyes that I might see the wonderful things that you have planned for me.
O Lord, you are what I need. For you are that I desire.

O Lord, let the fountain of your life flow into my inner most being.

O Lord, I need your unending love that reaches to the stars.

O Lord, open my heart and fill it with your perfect love and compassion and send me forth to your people.

O Lord, let your unending love flow like a mighty river unto me and fulfill all your perfect desires for my life. For your glory honour and praise.

The Lord was teaching me his divine ways and opening my eyes while using my vessel to do his perfect will. I was still a very hard headed individual that would still have to suffer many more things before I would come into the fullness of the Word of God. For the salvation of God is ongoing, line upon line, and precept upon precept.

Many a dark day still lay ahead me as this truth was being established in my heart. I still lacked much understanding about the discipline and the ways of the Lord in my life. Never mind the things that would be required of me in order that His perfect will might be done in life.

Chapter 11

THE WATER BROKE

It was shortly after the previous events that I had a spiritual encounter that would expose to me in no uncertain terms as to the validity of the spiritual realm. One night I began to pray and ask the Lord for open vision that I might see into the spiritual realm. I asked that He would just pull the corner back and allow me to look inside for just a moment.

I don't know whether or not I really believed in my heart that He would answer such a request. **_But of course He did._**

A friend had given me a small water bed and shortly after putting it together the heater went out so I had to sleep on the floor that night.

Sometime during the night I was awakened by blood curdling screams that seem to shake the whole house. As my eyes focused I saw 3 spirits hovering over the top of me. They were covered in torn rags and their faces were distorted and looked as though they were in great pain. I was so paralyzed that I could not move a muscle. I was shaken to the core of my being. The fear that I experienced was so great that I actually saw my spirit sit up as I was laying on the floor. This event lasted only a few seconds but it had nearly scared me to death.

As soon as it was over I sat up and was sick to my stomach. Where I had laid on the mattress there was an outline of my body in cold sweat. I immediately asked the Lord what had happened.

I heard the Lord respond, ***"these are the 3 spirits that have been assigned by the enemy to destroy your life. They are the spirits of murder, lust and suicide. The enemy has sent them from the pits of hell to destroy your soul and to rob you of your destiny, but you shall overcome."***

After that experience I would be very careful as to the things that I would ask the Lord to do for me when I prayed in the spirit. From this point forward the events in my life would unfold with brake neck speed. Several nights later I was awakened by a knock on my door it was an Atlanta Police officer that had been sent there by my ex-wife as I did not have a phone. He informed me that my grandmother was in Kennestone Hospital in Marietta in a coma and wasn't expected to live. I jumped up got dressed and started racing up 1-285 as fast as I could. Now, the only other person that had ever loved me was on her death bed and I would surely be alone when she left. Fear swept over my soul as I considered that I would never know human love again as there had been only one other love in my life and she had left me also. I contended that if she left I would be alone for the rest of my life.

As I passed Roswell road I was weeping so hard I could hardly see the road when I heard the voice of the Lord again, ***"Slow down my son, for I have kept her."***

I slowed down and wept all the way to the hospital crying out to God. I asked the Lord that if she had not given her life to him that he would give her one last chance and to use me if it pleased him.

I arrived at the hospital and went straightway to the ICU where I met my aunt Janis in the waiting room. I had to wait for the next visiting times to open before I could see her.

My grandmother had suffered a major stroke and massive heart attack. My aunt found her laying in the hall where she had been laying there for hours. The doctors said she had been in a deep coma since she arrived with no response at all.

This had happened on Friday morning and I was not informed by the Atlanta Police Dept. until around Sunday night around 2am. She had been motionless and on a ventilator with her blood pressure off the charts for nearly 3 days. When I got my chance to see her I was told that I could stay for only a few minutes. I walked in and over to her bedside and leaned over and kissed her on her forehead and whispered in her ear and said, Grandmother its okay I am here, just relax. I know that God has kept you so that I could see you one more time. All at once all the machines that she was connected to started going off and bells and whistles were screaming.

From behind me there came a flurry of activity as Doctors and Nurses stormed the room and began to throw the sheets back while checking the many machines that she was connected to. I turned and asked what was going on? The Doctor in charge said, we don't know, but her blood pressure just fell 60 points after not having moved for 3 days. I responded with I know why this is happening, the Lord is answering my prayers. The doctors responded, we do not care what the reason is, but if this is the result of your being in here you can come in as often as you want.

I left and went into the waiting room where I shared with my Aunt the amazing love of my God. She was amazed at what had just transpired and wanted to go back in with me the next time. About 2 hours later we went back in and again I walked over to her bedside kissed her as before and leaned over and started brushing her hair with my hand. I leaned over and whispered in her ear, I said Grandmother, I know that you can hear me and I know that you have lived your life in fear and pain, but the Lord has brought me here today to say some things to you.

Do you remember all those little talks we had recently? Well, today is the day, if you have not accepted the Lord as your Savior, now is the time. And as if on cue she opened her eyes and began to cry with tears running down her face onto her pillow, her eyes were focused on me.

And again the buzzers and bells on the machine started sounding. And once again all the doctors and nurses on the floor came in and began checking the machines as before. When they could not find anything wrong with the machines they stood there looking at me. I asked what was wrong and they responded, we do not know but her blood pressure has just fallen to normal.

I turned back to my Grandmother and continued to whisper in her ear while behind me the entire staff of the ICU stood in silence. As I spoke to her, I felt my soul being flooded with wave after wave of the love of God, just as I had experienced that morning in the mountains only a few months before. This amazing love of God came in wave after wave washing over me like a mighty river. As I whispered into her ear, I said that this was the love and mercy of God and that she should not be afraid. As I whispered these things to her my spiritual eyes were opened once again, and I saw a vision. I saw a vision of a little girl wearing a green dress printed with flowers and she was barefoot. I saw her coming over a hill with a field of beautiful flowers in front of her. She was dancing through this field and picking flowers one handful after another. As fast as she picked them they would grow and bloom again. I saw her with her arms full of the flowers of God and I saw the joy of the Lord was upon her face.

I said Grandmother, I see you in the garden of God where there is no more pain and suffering. It's okay now...It's time for you to go home and jump into the arms of Jesus. And with that she closed her eyes and never awoke again. I turned to see every doctor and every nurse including my aunt with tears on their faces and no one said a word. This experience deeply touched my aunt Janis and all that were on that day as they witnessed the love and mercy of Almighty God in a very special and profound way.

And once again He had heard my prayer and answered.

For the Lord had kept her for me.

The only other human that had touched my heart was gone and yet I was filled with an all knowing confidence that she was in heaven and moreover I would be ok…

I remembered how she would treat me as a child when we would go to visit her in Marietta. We would go to see her nearly every week and one Sunday I had acted up in the car and made my dad angry. When we arrived he told me to stay in the car as punishment and that I would not get to see her at all this visit. This broke my heart but his decision could not be altered. When the family went into her apartment she asked where is randy? My dad said, he is down in the car and wasn't coming up as punishment.

She said, well, if he isn't coming in I will go down and sit with him in the car!

And that's what she did. After a few minutes my dad came down and said that I could come up and visit with the rest of the family.

She loved me like a son. And I loved her very deeply.

Chapter 12

THE VISITATION

I was being healed by the hand of God through the avenue of pain and loss even as I said goodbye to a woman that I loved so deeply. I also knew that she was going on ahead into the Kingdom of God and into His love that endures forever and ever. It seemed to me at that time that my life experiences were running backwards as to the way one would think things should be in a spiritual journey. There were times that I thought of myself as a breach baby. My spiritual growth and development were coming to maturity as I walked out my beliefs by faith in action despite my feelings, fears, pain and misconceptions about the ways of God. ***This was a great revelation to me...***

James and Leann Eubanks a precious brother and sister in the Lord who had given me the old Toyota with the bullet holes just happened to live within a stone's throw behind the hospital on Lacy Street. So after the event in the ICU I went to their house and recounted to them my experience and asked if I could stay the night as I was very exhausted emotionally.

They were blessed with my testimony of the amazing love of our God they and gave me the keys to their home. I went onto the back porch and sat down and began to pour my heart out to the Lord, as I was so dumbfounded that this God could be so gracious and kind to me in the hour of my loss.

All I could do was sit there on their back porch floor and offer Him my tears as a sacrifice. I stayed there on the floor for several hours pouring my heart out to Him in thanksgiving for being so merciful to me, for giving me a few last moments with a woman whom I had loved so dearly and had made me feel special and wanted.

Once again, He had heard my supplications and had answered accordingly. I was so very grateful that that night I slept as though I was a newborn in my mother's arms. I was covered like a blanket in the peace of God all night. A peace that surpasses all understanding. Even though I had suffered a great loss I was at perfect peace. And through it all I was coming into an understanding that I was special to God as one of His children.

Around 9am the next morning I arose just in time to see James and Leann off to work. I sat down on the couch and with the morning sun rising over my shoulder I began to read a book titled " The Real Billy Sunday" by Elijah P. Brown which I still own today. As I began to read about this man who had some of the same experiences that I had, something wonderful began to happen to me. I had not gotten very deep into the book when I began to experience the Spirit of Lord in the same way that I experienced Him in the mountains many months before, only this time it was much more intense.

As I sat there I felt as though something warm and wonderful was being poured on top on my head and it ran to the souls of my feet. It began in short waves and then longer waves increasing in measure as they flowed over my entire body. As usual I began to weep from the very bottom of my being.

Not knowing as to the purpose for this visitation I arose and began to walk towards the kitchen. All the waves stopped, but as I leaned up against the kitchen wall and stood there in amazement as to what was transpiring the waves came again ever growing in intensity.

I walked through the whole and each time I moved the waves would stop and each time I stopped moving the waves would come growing ever stronger. I walked into the room where James had a piano and there I fell on my face pouring out my heart before my God saying through my tears, *"Stay your hand I can take no more!"*

Once again, I had found myself turning the corner in the presence of Almighty God, and this time His Holy presence filled the whole house so that I could not even stand.

I heard a gentle voice saying, ***"Today, I have healed your heart that was broken when you were a child. I am filling you with my Holy Spirit***

and I am commanding you to go forth and preach my Word and minister to the lost and broken hearted.

I broke out into song and began to praise Him lying there on the floor. For I could do nothing but lay there and be bathed in His mighty power and His amazing wonderful love.

Lift your voice and sing His praise.

Lift your voice and sing and shout before Him.

Let all the people dance before him.

Let every nation praise His Holy Name!

For Glory and Honor and Praise belongs to Him who alone can heal the human heart.

Lift your voice to Him for He is worthy to receive all the praise.

Who besides you O God, has the power to put a broken heart back together again?

Glory and Honor and Praise belongs to Him!

Chapter 13

DIPLOMAS AND DEGREES

W hile this experience was glorious and mighty and touched my heart deeply I would soon have to learn another very important lesson. Although I had heard directly from the Lord I would allow my un-renewed mind to convince me otherwise of the directives I had just received.

"No man knows the heart of man save the Spirit of God."

I would experience the presence of the Lord in a mighty way and turn right around and make mistakes that would make those that were seasoned in the Lord shake their heads in disbelief. My problem did not lay in a lack of desire to serve the Lord, no... But it lay in my mind that kept me rationalizing my decisions based on my limited understanding. This would cause me to resist the grace of God in my life. This resistance caused me to make many errors in judgment and would continue to cause me to suffer great pain. My will still had to be brought into full submission to the perfect will of God. And many more trials still awaited me in my journey to find my destiny in God. In some degree I did go forth and do those things that I had been commanded to do. I was asked to preach at different churches even in other states. I did try to walk in the things that I heard from the Lord. Even though I would succumb to the inner workings of my mind that said, because I was not educated and lacked the degrees necessary for ministry, that this lack fundamentally disqualified me from the Lord's service. Looking back now, I know that it was a lie from the enemy and was an attempt to render me ineffective and paralyze me from going forth by grace. I would have to come to a place in my walk with God that I could ignore the nay-Sayers that called my lack of education and academic worthiness into account.

I also had to face one of my greatest fears of stepping out into deep waters and trusting God in ever expanding faith. This fear would cause me to wander from the path and calling on my life and would have to be dealt with before any true ministry could take place.

Pastor Chuck Strong gave me many opportunities to walk in my calling over the years but I was very inconsistent in my walk with the Holy Spirit to have allowed anything of spiritual value from the Lord to have come forth. Yet through all my errors and rebellion the tender mercies of my Father in heaven remained unchanged towards me. His patient hand and longsuffering and eternal love continued to cover my life and my foot-steps.

"We can see only dimly and partly at best, but He who sees all sees the beginning, the middle and the end of our journey. It is His workmanship in our lives that He desires to reveal to the world. I thank Him to this day that He did not give up on the work of his hands. I thank Him that he did not cast down the work that He began in me. From the beginning I have truly put His love and mercy to the test. But with all my short comings I have found that His loving kindness and patience towards me reaches higher than the sky and goes to the deepest sea. And just as His great love endures forever, so does His desire to bring me into that amazing love and into full son ship. And His desire has never changed towards me.

I am thankful for His great love.
"For it is His loving kindness that leads us to repentance."

Faith is a spiritual muscle that has to be flexed daily if it is to remain strong and viable towards God. Fear of failure and the fear of man has no place in true faith and is a snare. For the faith that pleases God looks to the author and finisher of our faith and unto Him alone.

And His name is, **"Christ Jesus."**

In the early 90's I thought I could recapture something that I had lost many years before in my first marriage. I thought I was ready to be married again so I married a woman 12 years my junior who had been previously divorced with child.

I wanted to love her and do all the things that I had failed to do in my first marriage. But in less than a year the writing was on the wall and I could see yet another catastrophic event on the horizon.

I had gone ahead of the Lord yet again and had not inquired of Him by making a decision that would send me off onto a side path that would cost me dearly, not to mention the effect that it would have on the rest of my life.

Unless the Lord builds the house, its builders labor in vain. Psalms 127:1

And the foundation of the house that I was attempting to build would soon be blown apart.

This error in judgment would turn out to be one of my greatest victories veiled in the greatest darkness of my soul to date and cause me to grow abundantly in the things of God.

Chapter 14

I NEARLY MISSED MY STEP

The following event would eventually bring me ever closer to maturity and to submission to the will of God for my life. I was still living in Buckhead and playing softball on the church team and even ushering from time to time. I was working for a widow woman of Roswell Road doing a lot of remodeling on her home. In my weakness and lack of character I was over charging her for the work that I was doing. My desire and lack of trust in the Lord had caused me to try and to extricate myself from my poverty.

I was not willing to wait on the Lord to bring me into his prosperity. This blindness left me unaware of the depth of my corruption and how it had affected my integrity, what little I had left of it anyway.

All this had set the stage for the rapid set of events that would soon take place in my life. And the time table for these events would consume the next 7 years of my life.

One day she met me at the front door and said that she had been praying for me and that the Lord and given her only one word with regards to me.

She said the word was **"flagrant"** and she said that Lord had told her that I would know what it meant.

And I did.

She asked me to finish the work that I had started by cutting down the large dogwood tree closest to the house. Ignoring the word I had just received I asked her if I could tend to the tree and to see if I could save it. She agreed.

I did this for the additional work that would ensue not because I had some special affinity for the tree although it was old and had produced a lot of color in the past. As I began to work I found out that it was nearly 50 years old. The tree had fungus growing on its trunk and up into its limbs. Many of the branches were already dead or were dying. I climbed up into the tree with my saw and steel brush and began to scrape and trim away the damage. As I sat on a limb and worked I heard a voice that came from the base of the tree below me.

And the voice said, "If this tree could speak, what do you think it would be saying right now?"

Without hesitation having heard this voice many times before and knowing it to be the voice of the

Lord, I responded out loud not caring one whit if anyone over heard me. "I said, it would probably be asking why I was cutting off its branches and scraping off the damage to its trunk. But if I do not do these things it will die and have to be cut down.

The Lord said, that is correct. Do you think that this tree feels pain from the work that you are doing to save its life?

I said, yes of course it does and it would probably be screaming in pain, but if I do not address these things it will surely die.

And again the Lord said, that is correct, and to the same degree that you have tended to this tree so shall I tend unto you so that you might produce fruit for my glory."

I did not know then what lay ahead of me so that I might walk in the fulfillment of those words. Only a few months later on the heels of yet another divorce I would find myself in another major crisis. One night just before this crisis was to peak I had a dream that was the night mare of all nightmares. It was so real in its emotions that it caused me to sit up in the bed screaming at the top of my lungs causing my wife to literally freak out beside me. I sent my wife to Texas to see her dying mother and I went to the mountains to visit an old friend.

I just had to get away...

He lived up in Talking Rock Georgia so far back in the woods that I had to forge a creek to get to his house. When I arrived we went out and fired some rifles at targets off his deck. Before I left he offered me one of his rifles from his collection. It was a model 1948 .303 British Enfield bolt action that belonged to his wife. When she found out that he had given it to me she went ballistic to say the very least. In looking back I now know that it wasn't just his wife raising objection to my having that rifle, but it was also the Spirit of the Lord. Despite all the hollering and screaming objections I took the rifle home anyway.

When I got back to Atlanta I tore it down completely to refinish it and put it in a box on top of the china cabinet. My wife came home from Texas and as soon as she walked through the door we began to argue and scream at each other. A longtime friend of hers was getting married in West Virginia and we had been invited. On the way home from the wedding we fought like cats and dogs to the point that I got out of the van in Tennessee and said that I would walk the rest of the way. I was so depressed and despondent knowing that very soon this would end in another major life failure.

When we got home she went out to party at some clubs and I went to one of my contract jobs to work. I came home around 1am only to find the house empty. When she came home she went straight way to bed and slammed the door. After a few minutes I went into the bedroom and laid down next to her and asked her to forgive me for my behavior earlier in the day. She told me that if I thought that all I had to do was come into her bedroom acting like a whipped puppy and ask for her forgiveness and that she would grant it... that I had it all wrong, that it did not work that way mister! After hearing that I slipped off my wedding band and laid it next to her on my pillow and left the room. I went down the hallway and took the rifle off the top of the china cabinet and sat down and began putting it back together again.

When I had finished I put one shell in the chamber and loaded it. I sat down on the couch and placed the butt of the rifle between my shoes and push the barrel up under my chin.

I aimed the shot so that it would track through the center of my face and out the top of my head. As I sat there I knew that I had come full circle again and was facing one of the three demons that God had told me had been assigned to my life and rob me of my destiny.

But I did not care about those words I just wanted to end this miserable existence as fast as possible. I could not face another failure and all the associated pain of another divorce.

I pulled the trigger.

The rifle went off and my ears began to ring on a scale like I had never heard before with the over sound of water pouring down which I thought was my own blood pouring off my face. All I could do was sit there and shake my head... in total disbelief.

I could not believe that I could even fail at suicide on this scale. When would I ever learn that my life did not belong to me? After a few minutes I got up and walked back to the bedroom door which was now locked and I knocked on the door. She answered and I said, I think that I have really done it this time. You might want to call the EMS. And I turned and started back down the hall, she grabbed ahold of my arm that had copious amount of blood running down and onto the floor. I snatched myself away from her as I arrived at my desk, I reached for my bible and turned to,

Mark Chapter 14:21 where it says,
But woe to the man that betrays the Son
of Man! It would have been better for him
he had not been born.

With my blood running down my arm I underlined it! Then I went over and sat down and waited for the EMS to arrive. In my mind I believed that I betrayed Him by taking advantage of the widow woman and the failure of yet another relationship. I deserved to die. I wanted to love her and give her all the things that she needed and wanted. But one person can't give to another person if they don't have the capacity to contain the offering. My desire was genuine and sincere and her rejection struck a death blow to the center of my being and what I believed was the purest thing that I had to offer anyone.

I felt that if I failed here believing with all my heart that I had no chance of ever coming to victory in any other area of my life. I was damned if I did, and damned if I didn't.

When the EMS squad arrived they walked in carrying their emergency bags and turned and saw me sitting on the couch and they dropped their bags and just stared at me. It took 5 of them to get me on the stretcher and carry me down to the ambulance as I weighed around 225lbs and was very stout. Never mind the fact that I wanted to walk out and not be carried out. I could not communicate with them at all as I did not know the extent of the damage to my face.

Much later I would come to know that what I thought was blood running down my face was actually water from the roof. The bullet had passed through the center of my face and out between my eyes. Then it travelled through the sheetrock ceiling and blew a hole in the flat asphalt roof allowing the rain water to pour in on the couch.

Upon arrival at Shallowford Hospital I was rushed into the ER where I sat on the edge of the bed and with my vision failing I could see every Doctor and nurse and candy stripper on staff that night crowded into that room trying to get a look at me. I was given paper and pen and I answered questions before going into emergency surgery.

One of the last things I remember before I lost my vision was Pastor Chuck standing in the hallway as I was rushed back into surgery and the expression of sadness on his face.

This was the beginning of a long journey of discovery into the depths of my soul and into the deep things of God. I was in a very deep place and the deep in me was calling out to the deep in God. What seemed to be on the surface a tragedy of deadly proportions would one day by the Grace and Mercy of God be turned into one my greatest triumphs.

And we know that in all things God works for the good of those who love him and who are called according to his purpose. Romans: 8:28

And we know that no weapon formed against us shall prosper. And those that raise up against me shall fall. I will not fear what the devil may bring against me.

For I am a servant of God!

I knew that I had been called of God and in the coming years through this experience I would finally answer that call with all my heart, soul, mind and strength and begin to flow in the Spirit of God for His glory honour and praise.

I spent 10 days at Shallowford Hospital before I was transferred to Grady Memorial Hospital because I did not have any insurance. The Hospital Administrator approached my mother and told her that with the seriousness of my injuries that the total cost so far had exceeded $85,000 and could easily go into the millions of dollars. While there at Shallowford I had over 12 major plastic surgeries with 2 of them being 15 hour surgeries back to back.

My face had been completely destroyed with the upper maxilla and lower mandible blown into pieces nearly back to the hinge. The bullet had travelled through the center of my palate impacting my nose and both cheek bones and both eye sockets.

The bone base that created the orbits that held my eyes in place would have to be rebuilt with bone grafts from my skull.

My nose was 90% destroyed along with all my gums. Most of my teeth had been blown away and the ones I did not lose had been blasted upwards into my skull and the sheetrock ceiling.

The bullet had split my face open completely even so that you could see the spinal cord in the back of my throat. My head had swelled 3 to 4 times its normal size from the gun powder and the infection that followed. My eyes were temporally placed in the place where the eye sockets had been and bandaged closed. In order to breathe I had a tracheotomy installed in my throat and with it a series of drainage tubes to relieve the pressure on my brain. For all intents and purposes I was blind and unable to speak one audible word. The doctors there basically sent me down the road to Grady to die. It was just that bad.

Amazingly with all the damage to my face interiorly as well as exteriorly the bullet had not pierced my tongue. The way the bullet tracked through my mouth and its exit between my eyes, it is only a true miracle of God that not one stitch was put into my tongue. The doctors there could not offer any explanation on the entrance and exit, only to say, ***it had to be divine intervention.***

Upon my arrival at Grady Memorial there was no room me and I was placed in the hallway in the basement near the morgue. My mother stood by my side with my transfer papers and x-rays. And there I waited on the dock with a half dozen pieces of medical equipment. After about 3 hours in the hallway I heard a Hospital representative approached my mother and ask her did she have all my paper work.

She said, yes I do and she handed the paper work to him. He responded no... Mrs. Rogers you do not understand. Your son is going to die... for there is nothing that can be done for him here at Grady his injury is too severe. You need to gather together all the paperwork for his funeral and burial etc. The hospital representative went on to say I am so very sorry, but even if he did live he will be blind and unable to speak.

I might have been blind and unable to speak but I heard those words and laying there I thought to myself, if I was going to die I would have died when the rifle went off back at the apartment not down here on some hospital dock. Eventually I was admitted into the hospital and moved to an upper floor ICU where many more surgeries would follow.

I had so many medical devices attached to me that I was placed in a private room to await the surgery schedule. The next morning I met Doctor Robert Wood and his associate whose name escapes me now. They were both out of Emory University Medical Center who would be greatly used by God to help me to a place restoration. Both of them set me up for a series operations that would lay the foundational work for future surgeries that would bring back to a place of normalcy.

In our first meeting I was told that I would have to agree to sign off on each and every surgery and release all doctors and the Hospital of any liability, as they were going to operate on me using experimental techniques that had never been done before. I agreed and the operations began in earnest.

At first I was not treated very well by the staff and nurses while I was at Grady Memorial. I could not communicate with them and they did not want to communicate with me as they came in to treat me and do what was required. I was turned over and cleaned, given shots without one word being spoken. I would lay there in total darkness 24 hours a day waiting for a doctor or nurse to come in on their morning rounds. This would be the only interaction outside the few visitors that would come to see me. No one asked how I was doing or if I needed anything and even if they had how would I have conveyed it to them?

Chapter 15

2.3 MILLION RECONSTRUCTION

This gave me plenty of time to be introspective and assess my situation and the things that had brought me to this place. I was alone in my darkness with only one place and one person to turn to and find my deliverance and healing. I was alone with God and He was there with me. I again began to cry out from the deepest part of my being not making one audible sound. I knew that He would hear my cry and answer me. I had hit the rock hard bottom of my life and I could only cry out to the Great Creator for help.

I knew that if I were to walk out of that hospital it would be by His grace and mercy.

And walk out of that hospital I would.

Day after day I laid there waiting for a nurse to inform me that I had been scheduled for a surgery the next day. I would only be informed the night before and with it all the preparation that goes with it. I went into the hospital on Feb. 28th 1992 weighing somewhere around 225lbs to 250lbs and by March 25th I had lost down to 155lbs. I was dying of starvation never mind the multiple operations that were removing literally pounds of my flesh and bone to close up the opening in my face. For surgery after surgery was failing due to the massive infections that were destroying any attempt to restore my face.

After many reconstructive surgeries I had been give some vision in my right eye and with it double and triple vision. One morning I was awakened by a nurse in ICU that said that I had a visitor waiting for me in the hall. She went on to say that he had been waiting on me to wake up for hours. I could not speak but nodded to her and she went and let him into the unit.

In came an aged gentleman probably in his 80's whom I did not know and had never met. He immediately took my hand and squeezed it tightly as he knelt beside my bed. He said, Randall, look at me! So I turned to look with the only eye I had to see with. He said again, Randall, I said look at me! And when I looked at him in his eyes, I saw a ring of fire and in the center of that ring of fire a man dressed in a long white robe. This man said that he had been asked to come and pray for me. He began to pray and the entire time that he prayed all I could see was the ring of fire in his eyes and the man dressed in white.

Then he shouted, ***Randall! This is not unto death! You will recover and serve the Lord!***

This man came to visit me 2 times and each time that he prayed I felt the power and love of God.

Later I would come to find out that the man who had come to see me was the Senior Retired Pastor of Mt Paran Church of God. Dr. McCluen.

This experience would come to profoundly affect my attitude while in ICU. As I laid there thinking on the reasons why all these surgeries had failed and the fact that I was losing weight so rapidly. I knew that faith in God would have to again play its part if I were to have victory.

The next morning I awoke to hear a group of Doctors standing next to my bed speaking to a boy of about 17yrs who had done the same thing that I had done. I heard the doctors tell him that there was nothing else that could be done for him that he would be blind for the rest of his life.

I would lay there in my bed and night after night watch death come into the ICU and claim its victims. One after another I watched and heard the sounds of death and saw the sheets pulled up over people in that place. And I knew that I had to get focused and find my way out...

Chapter 16

AN ASPIRIN A DAY

D ue to the amount of damage that had been done to my face I had been placed on the hardest pain medications available. But from the moment the rifle went off I had not experienced one gram of pain. The explanation for this I believe goes back to the conversation at the dogwood tree that I was tending to for the widow woman only a few months before. Everyone assumed that I had to be in great pain but I wasn't for His word to me that day gave me great peace in my darkest hour. It was His great mercy and abiding unfathomable peace that had rescued me.

I needed no pain medications at all!

I would spend hours on my back listening to the sounds of people talking and walking up and down the hallway. This would only be interrupted when a nurse would come into my room to pump 1 or 2 cans into my feeding tube every 5 or 6 hours or so.

This went on for weeks and I progressively grew weaker until one night I decided to take matters into my own hands and I started to exercise my legs by placing them through the rails on the bed and started stretching them back and forth.

One morning just before the doctors came into my room for my morning consultation and check-up. I decided to try and stand up on what I thought were my new legs. I threw my legs over the side of my bed and when my feet hit the floor, I remember standing there for all of 10 seconds before doing a 180 passing out hitting my head on the table that was between the beds.

When I came to I was berated by the Doctors for what they called a stupid stunt as they attended to the stiches in my head. I wrote on a piece of paper the best that I could, that I felt that I had to start and try to get up because if didn't I was going to die of starvation. They responded by saying, not to mention the fact that we can't operate on you until you get stronger and something is done about all these infections.

After a long discussion they said if I were able to hold onto my Christmas tree that held all my medications that I could walk the halls as much as I could handle it. And walk I did…At first with the help of a nurse but I was soon on my own. I would walk the halls pushing my Christmas tree all night even though I had double and triple vision I walked.

Jeff Benoit a brother in the Lord brought me a cassette player and a nurse would load it with worship music mostly by Phil Driscoll. I would walk the hall all night long singing songs of praise and thanksgiving to the Lord. Never making a sound least ways a sound that anyone in ear shot could understand. A symphony of praise rose up from deep within my soul unto my God and my King. I would walk past the nurse's station to the end of the floor from the time the visitors left till just before the doctors came in for their rounds the next morning.

One morning just after the doctors had made their rounds I was trying to sleep when I heard a knock at my door. A nurse that had been on duty that night stuck her head in and asked if she could come into my room. I nodded yes and in behind her came 3 other nurses who were going off duty also.

She came to my bedside and said, I know you can't speak but we know that God is with you. We want to pray and have you agree with us as we pray aloud. We see the power of God working mightily in your life and this has witnessed to us greatly. They prayed for their children and families respectfully. And when they had finished I touched them each on their foreheads and nodded in agreement in Christ Jesus Name.

Once again, the Lord was bringing his people to me just as he had promised me in the mountains. The Lord is faithful to see His word accomplish what it was sent forth to do.

And it will not return to him void.

From that day forward my relationship with the nurses would change for the better. If I needed paper and pen to communicate they saw that I had plenty. I requested several extra cans of Sustacal because I was still hungry after the morning feeding. The next morning I had several cases of different flavors stacked up against the wall. I now could drink all I wanted whenever I wanted. And drink I did. I was being renewed.

I would pump 5 to 6 cans at a time and the weight that I had lost came roaring back. My walls looked like Costco with chocolate and vanilla double stacked deep. Now I was ready to move forward and continue with my operations.

He is worthy to be praised!

Praise the Lord, O my soul, all my inmost being, praise his holy name. Praise the Lord, O my soul and forget not his benefits, who forgives you all your sins and heals all your diseases, who redeems your life from the pit and crowns you with love and compassion, and satisfies your desires with good things so that your youth is renewed like the eagles Psalms 103:1-5

Up to that day most of my surgeries had failed due to infections and lack of blood flow. My entire body was being used for bone, skin, tissue artery, blood vessels and I was running out of viable donor sites. Things would have to change and quickly or the reconstruction would come to an abrupt halt. Then I remembered the words of the old preacher that came to see me. Randall, this is not unto death! You shall recover and serve the Lord!

Laying on my bed one night just before the surgeries were to start up again, I was talking to the Lord on the inside and I came to ask Him a question.

Lord, why are all these surgeries failing due to infections and if this was not unto death then why have I not recovered?

The Lord spoke to me and said, ***"The reason that the work has failed is because you have not purposed in your heart to live for me and do my perfect will."***

I said, okay I agree with you and tonight I repent of my unbelief and my rebellion. I purpose this day to live and to live for and you alone for your glory, honour and praise. The next morning I was scheduled for a surgery, so I wrote a short letter for the doctor to read. I was prepped for surgery and wheeled into the OR with the note folded up like a scroll in my hand. And just before they were to put me to sleep I reached out and grabbed his surgical gown. Dr. Dostel leaned over to me and said, Randall, are you ready to try this again? I raised the note for him to see and he said that he could not touch it as he was already sterile. But he asked one his assistants to come over and unfold it for him. She held it as he began to read it aloud.

Chapter 17

SUCCESS AT LAST!

The note read, Dear Doctor Dostel, The reason that all these surgeries have failed to this point has been due to my not having purposed in my heart to live and to live for God. Last night I purposed in my heart to do just that to His glory, honor and praise. And the Lord has promised me success. From this point forward every surgery will be a success in the Name of Jesus Christ.

As one of the nurses held the note he read it aloud and said, all of us standing here today agree with you, in the Name of Jesus Christ. I looked around the OR and everyone there looked back at me and said out loud that they agreed.

I went to sleep and awoke with exactly what I had asked for, I had success for the first time in 24 operations. The previous 24 operations had only accomplished in removing pounds of tissue and bone grafts that had failed miserably.

The damage to my face was so severe that tissue had to be removed from my stomach to lay a foundation for new gums and tissue to cover the bone grafts. A free flap was taken from my arm to begin the base for my new nose and to close the grapefruit size hole in my face. Part of that operation helped close up what was once my palate leaving only a sliver dollar opening to this date. A 22 inch incision was made on my hip where a major section of my hip bone was removed to rebuild my upper and lower jaw. Part of my sternum was removed along with several ribs to start my nose reconstruction. Many small arteries and small blood vessels were donated from different areas of my body and grafted into my face to rebuild my lips. Steel plates, screws and wire were used to pull my face back together again.

A large free flap from my right leg was removed to help close the opening in my face. Everything the doctors did on me during my time at Grady Memorial Hospital was unorthodox and experimental at best. But I did not worry and I had no fear because I had the word of my God in my heart. And I was holding on to His word for dear life.

For it was my life.
For He is my life.

While at Grady I spent most of my time in ICU. Even after my surgeries I would have to be monitored before being able to go to the floor. And even though I was not in any pain from the gunshot I did experience some pain and discomfort from the additional surgeries and grafts and etc. But what pain or discomfort that I experienced did not warrant the over kill of pain medication that they were pumping into me daily.

The pain medications kept me from sleeping and would eventually cause me great pain. After one specific surgery I was unable to sleep for over 3 days and nights. Being unable to speak and communicate this to anyone except the nurses that came on duty that I knew, I was left to myself and the lack of concern by those that did not know me. If I did not have paper and pen I could not tell anyone how I was feeling or if I needed anything. I laid there in the ICU for days trying to sleep but the pain medications would only let me relax down to a point and then aggravate me to no end. I had lost all connection with time and reality after this specific surgery and I felt that I was about to lose my mind. Hour after hour I laid there hearing the sounds of footsteps and voices, doors opening and closing, buzzers and bells all magnified 100 fold. And I was experiencing all this because of the drugs that I did not need.

I began to tap on the bed rail to get the attention of the male nurse on duty. And the first few times he did come to my bedside and ask me what I wanted. I made the sign like I needed to write and he went and brought me a pen and paper and to the best of my ability with only one eye and double vision I wrote my note to him. I told him that I was about to lose it mentally because I had not been able to sleep for over 3 days. I told him that if I did not get some sleep that I was going to get up out of that bed pull out all these tubes and go home.

He told me, you ain't going nowhere Mister Rogers. **Now go to sleep!**

This went on for several hours and soon worked up into a full blown episode when he screamed at me from across the room and said that he was not coming over to my bedside again.

He said, **GO TO SLEEP AND LEAVE ME ALONE!**

Tell your problems to the doctors in the morning when they make their rounds. I tried with all my heart but I was being tormented with the sounds of the hospital.

So I sat up and did exactly what I said that I would do... I sat up and started disconnecting all the tubes and the main artery lines. This caused blood and fluids of all kinds to start pumping on the floor, my bed and the walls. All total I was connected to at least 20 machines and with fluid and medications and drainage lines being pumped all over the floor as I made my plans to go home. I had had enough.

The ICU was filled with all kinds of buzzers, bells and alarms and nurses and doctors came from everywhere and I was rushed back into the OR for over 5 hours to reattach everything that I had torn out.

Even the strongest man among us will lose it after 3 days of no sleep especially under the influence of opiate based drugs. I had been placed on a slow morphine drip plus a whole host of other drugs because they thought I needed it. The doctors asked me the next day why I had done such a thing. Was this another attempt to take your life? I told them that I had had 3 days of no sleep and it was due to the drugs and sleep deprivation that caused the event. In fact, I was not in any pain and I felt that I did not need the drugs that they were giving me despite what they may have concluded? I told them that I no longer wanted any pain medication unless I specifically made a request for pain medication.

They agreed and said that from that day forward that I was off all pain medications and that it would be noted on my chart and I would not receive any unless I requested them.

And I did not request any opiate pain medication from that day forward.

A few days later I found myself back with the same male nurse that I had the day of my attempted escape. He came over to my bedside and said, Well, Well, here you are again. I just wanted you to know that that little stunt that you pulled the other day cost me several hours of overtime and lots of paperwork. I want to tell you some things about life here in the ICU. When you hear that alarm go off and the intercom goes off asking for Dr.99 that means that someone has gone into cardiac arrest in the ICU.

People in here die every day and every night. It is no big deal and Mister Rogers, tonight is your night. Do you see the rubber bags that are attached to your drainage lines? It is my job to drain those bags when they fully expand having been filled with fluid.

These bags have to be drained every hour or so, and If they are not drained the fluid will back up and begin to flow back into your lungs and you will drown on your own fluid.

And tonight, I will not drain your bags and you will die.

With that he pushed my bed and all my equipment into a side room that only had chairs and spare beds stacked to the ceiling. I was in a room all alone except for the one light over the sink and a clock on the wall. I had been placed in a metal tub on several sheets and blankets and tied down through the wash out ports because the staff still believed that I was a threat to myself. I was bound by my ankles and my wrists with strips of cloth unable to move one inch and unable to speak one word. I was told that this was for my own protection as many of my veins had collapsed and could not stand a second event like the first. I had one large drainage bag under each arm and at least one for my head and probably more. As I laid there I could feel the bags doing their job and the swelling had begun when the nurse came back into my room. He stood at the head of my bed/tank and leaned over and said, these bags will fill quickly and after you have drowned I will come in and drain them just before the doctors make their rounds. I will come in clean you up change your sheets and no one will know what happened to you.

Your case is closed… He left the room.

I laid there thinking, O Man, all I wanted to do was sleep a few hours not the rest of my life. So, again I started talking to the Lord and said, Well, here I am again Lord. It seems that when I am not trying to destroy myself, there are those who are trying to do it for me.

Again, if I was going to die I would have died when the rifle went off.

I am not going to die now and not here!

Lord, how am I going to get through this?

The Lord answered me and said, I am the God of the elements. I am the God that created the elements, and they cannot take your life unless I give my word. I created you in the womb filled with fluid and you breathed life. Do not be afraid for I am with you. I am your Life!

As I laid there I began to experience wave after wave of the peace of God flooding my soul just like I had experienced in the mountains. I could not move a muscle or utter a word to deliver myself. I was a prisoner in what the enemy meant to be my death bed, yet I was at perfect peace.

I was lucid and very aware of what was going on around me as I had been off pain medications for over three days. I watched the clock on the wall as the hours passed and the bags began fill and began to drain back into my lungs. I turned my eyes to the ceiling and said from my heart, Lord, I trust you with my life.

What have I to dread. What have I to fear?

Leaning on the everlasting arms.
I have blessed peace with my Lord so near.
Leaning on the everlasting arms.
Safe and secure from all alarms.
Leaning on His everlasting arms

From that point forward it only took a few minutes and I could feel my lungs filling to overflowing and my breathing became more labored and shallow until I stopped breathing altogether. I knew that my lungs were full as I could hear and feel the fluid gurgling in my trach tube and collecting in volume in my throat. It was just then that I saw two beings dressed in brilliant white garments appear in the room. Both of them entered the room and stood beside my bed holding a single large silver ladle. For the next several hours they each took turn dipping their ladle into my chest and pouring its content into a container. The next morning just before daylight they departed as quickly as they had entered. I had watched them the entire night not being able to see their faces and not having said one word to me the entire visit.

I looked up at the clock on the wall and it was 6:51 am and I knew that the Doctors would soon be in to see me. Just then the nurse came into my room and leaned over my bed expecting to find me dead. He was very surprised to say the least to see that I was still with the living.

He threw the covers back to see if the bags had ruptured and the fluid had soaked my bedding. When he found that I was as dry as when he left me the night before, he became very disturbed and left the room.

A few moments later he returned and stood at the head of my bed/tank with his head directly over mine and with tears streaming down his face and falling onto my face in a broken voice he said, Mister Rogers, please forgive me I did not know what I was doing.

From the expression on his face I could tell that he was very disturbed and nearly in a full blown panic. I looked up into his eyes and I nodded in the affirmative.

He left…

I never saw him again in ICU or anywhere else in the hospital for that matter from that day forward. I did not say anything to the Doctors that morning and never said anything to anyone until I wrote about it here. After all, I was in there for attempting suicide and how much weight would be given to me on such a matter. The truth is, that I never felt it was that important and the Lord certainly never gave me any indication that it was his will to reveal this event to the hospital officials, so I kept it to myself.

All I knew was that my God was near to me. He had kept his word and He had kept my life again. I learned that night that no man can take my life unless my Lord gives his permission. I also learned that He held my life in His mighty hands and that I did not have to fear anything, anyone, not even death.

My God is a great God!
My God is a great God!

My God is mighty and in His hands he holds my very life.
My God is Great God!

As the weeks past I grew stronger and stronger and the schedule for my surgeries increased to the point that I was having a reconstructive surgery every 30 days. I was being operated on as fast as I could recover and this was to the amazement of all the doctors that worked on me. Since the pain medication problem had been dealt with I was even allowed to be fully awake during some of the procedures. I would watch via a mirror on several major operations which is almost unheard of in the medical community. I would be given a local and the doctor would talk to me through the entire procedure. This helped me greatly as I did not have to go to recovery and deal with coming out of the anesthesia medication.

When I would go for my consultations prior to the surgery date to discuss the upcoming procedure, I was told on many occasions that I was miracle of God and that everyone involved was in amazement as to how fast I completely recovered.

Several doctors said that I was one in a million and that a smaller man would not have fared as well as I had. I knew that it was much more than what they had concluded. I knew it was the everlasting amazing love and mercy of the God who loved my soul.

***O give thanks to the Lord for His love
endures forever!***
***O give thanks to the Lord for His love
endures forever!***
Forever and forever!

I would go to my consultations with a group of 3 to 4 doctors at a time some of which came from Emory University and others came from other countries such as England, Germany, and France and as far away as Australia. On one meeting I met a doctor from Israel and after the meeting as I was headed for the door he spoke to me a final word and said, Randall, God bless you!

I stumbled as those words hit my back with great power, as I turned I looked into his eyes and it was as though he could see the grace and mercy of God that was working in my life. And he was acknowledging that fact by blessing me with those words. When I looked back he smiled and nodded at me and we both knew what had happened.

Until that day no man had ever spoke such powerful words over my life with such an affect. God had placed his people in my life to speak his blessings over me that I might continue to move forward towards my destiny in Christ Jesus.

That is the love of God.

I was well on a journey that would last more than 5 to 7 years and consist of more than 50 to 100 reconstructive surgeries with 100's of hours of anesthesia. I was now strong enough to leave the hospital and go home. I would have to return many times in the coming months but now the basic foundations had been laid for my recovery.

When I arrived back at home things went from bad to worse as my wife could not deal with the disfigurement and my emotional adjustments. I was having problems trying to adjust to a new way of living, communicating as well as taking care of myself. In addition to everything on our plates my wife was pregnant and due any day. I had gotten out of the hospital in June of 1992 and she was due in July. I still had a whole hosts of unresolved issues and having relocated 50 miles south of Atlanta did not make things any better. And she wanted a divorce to boot.

My 3rd son was born July 5th and I was in the delivery room when he came into this world. I was asked to wear blue scrubs with a hair cap, this went well with the blue surgical mask that I had to wear when I went out into public. When Benjamin J. Quinton Rogers came into this world and the doctor woke him he began to cry and was immediately handed to me where he stopped crying to the amazement of all that were there that day. I held him close to my heart and he became very quiet. The doctors looked at each other and said that is not normal. I believe that it was a sign to me that the love of the Father abided in me and my son felt the peace of God.

My life was changing as I walked down the path of God. I had tried to destroy myself and at every turn God met me with His mighty power to save me and to bless me and to keep me headed towards my destiny.

I knew that I had to walk through these things so that I could identify with Him in his sufferings. For unless we know him in His sufferings we cannot know Him in His glory. God uses pain and suffering in the earth for this reason and it is a lifelong process.

Let it be said here that this all knowing and loving God did not do these things to me but used my bad decisions and wrong judgments to reveal Himself to me in the midst of my chaos. Our spiritual journey here on earth can be summed up this way; we are all searching for our Father in heaven whether we are aware of it or not. We are lost and stumbling in the darkness trying everything and anything that we can find to try and fill that place that can only be filled with the revelation of His perfect everlasting love. For He created that secret place for himself alone.

And once we have tasted that everlasting love we cannot be satisfied when anything else here on the earth. It is the revelation of this love in our inner most parts that will change us forever and ever. We are changed from the inside out. And now we become an open book for men to read of the mercy, grace and amazing love of the Ancient One.

And from that moment forward all we want is to abide forever in that revelation as we are held in His mighty arms close to his heart.

This is the purpose that He sent His only begotten Son to the Cross so that He could reestablish this intimate relationship with that which He had created in His likeness and image.

This is true Christianity.

In your presence that is where I belong.

O Lord my God, I want to live in your presence.

In your presence, seeking your holy face touching your grace

O Lord my God, in your presence is where I belong.

In your presence that is where I am strong.

I delight in your presence O Lord.

You are my strength and my song

I am your child and you are my God

In your presence I am loved.

And you call me by name.

It is not just knowing with our intellect that God has a people for having read it in the bible and that he bestows that love on them. This everlasting love must be shed abroad in our hearts by the work of the blessed Holy Spirit. And we come into this truth through the fires and tribulations here on earth until we are united when Him in spirit and truth.

As I sit here trying to rewrite this book I am even more aware today of how much He desires to reveal this truth to those who wander even now in darkness. I would like to say that this is an instant process one time and done. But the truth is that it is a continuous unfolding of the depth of this revelation to our soul. He told me many years ago that,

"He was going to make me an example of His patience, longsuffering and his love to his people, and they would know that He is the Lord thy God."

We will spend eternity searching the height, the width, and the length and depth of this love in Christ Jesus.

I have spent my entire life running from the very thing that I needed more than anything else in my life. It is from this place of rest that we find our true destiny and purpose. When we stop running He is able to pour over into us all the things that we have striven for and failed to achieve in our own strength.

What is the perfect will of God if not to be brought into an intimate relationship with Him through His Holy Son having been made holy and pure through his perfect and pure blood on the Cross; and to be made to sit in our rightful position in His Kingdom high and above all living things?

This then, is the Good, the Glad, the Merry News that causes a man to leap and to dance for joy. When this truth takes root deep in our soul there is joy inexpressible that bubbles up from the very deepest part of our being and an excitement about our new life and the future God has for us in Christ Jesus.

This is the good news that will cause us to leap and dance for joy when we experience the manifestation of the love of God, when He is pleased to pour himself over into our hearts.

Taste and see that the Lord is good.

We will give our everything even our very hearts to Him who gave the very best that He had to offer when this truth becomes a living reality in our hearts. We will sing and dance for joy when we see Him who created the universe hold us in his mighty arms and bathe us in his love.

When I got to this part of the book I remembered a poem that I wrote many years ago. Ironically I wrote it on a 1948 model type writer which was the same model year of the rifle I used. 1948 was the year that Israel was proclaimed to be a sovereign nation. I wrote this poem within a few days of beginning my journey to find my Father.

It was one of the first things that I wrote about Him and to him.

My nights were filled with despair and gloom as I knelt in the dark.
A rough and deep longing voice crying out to God seeking His holy and pure heart.
A gentle voice spoke saying, "Be still and know that I am God."
All that darkness departed with haste from that tiny room.
A glorious, glorious, wonderful light enveloped me like the wings of a snow white dove protecting his young.
A gentle voice spoke again saying, "Be still my son and receive my love."
Hebrews 4:12 The Word of God is living and active, sharper than a double edged sword, it penetrates even to the dividing

the soul and spirit, joints and marrow, it judges the thoughts and attitudes of the heart.

My heart was still being divided and my thoughts were still being exposed by the Word of God in my life. Shortly after my son was born I again found myself coming to another crisis situation. Notwithstanding all that I experienced in the mercy and grace of God I was still coming into the fullness of that revelation. I was changing on the inside even though on the outside my life looked like total chaos and a full on train wreck. I became very despondent for no matter how I tried to fix my marriage it would end in divorce. I lost control and took everything that I owned and piled it up in the back yard and poured gas on it.

This caused my wife to leave and call the Sherriff to intervene in the circumstance. There was a standoff in my driveway with the Sherriff and several duties.

I told them by writing notes that I had had enough of the ways things were going in my marriage and if they wanted me they would have to come and get me.

And of course they did...

They broke down the back door and came in in force with their hands on their weapons they surrounded me in the dining room. I wrote to them that as they could see I had some serious problems and as I saw it they had 3 choices. Take me to jail, take me to a mental hospital, or shoot me. The choice was theirs but one way or the other I was going to get out of this mess. The Sherriff said, we will take you to a mental hospital.

And with that I nodded in the affirmative and turned around where I was placed in handcuffs. I was taken straightway to Parkway Medical Center in Douglasville Georgia. I was signed in for 30 days for mental evaluation and locked up on the psyche ward. As soon as I arrived I was diagnosed manic depressive and place on Zoloft.

Because of my disfigurement I was allowed to take my medication back to my room each morning. I would stand over the toilet and say to the Lord from my heart, "drugs are not the solution to my problems." I did this every day that I was in Parkway Medical Center.

The staff would have classes nearly every day, some were one on one and others were in a group setting. It is important to note here that once again I had made a bad decision but God was about to use it and turn it around for his glory.

And we know that in all things God works for the good of those who love him, who are called according to his purpose. Romans 8:27-28

The staff would try and address the issues that had brought us to the Medical Center. I would sit there not being able to speak but listen to the myriad of reasons why these men and women had crashed and burned in their lives. I listened as they discussed their emotional problems and the pain had become so overwhelming that they could no longer manage it and could not escape from it.

After 4 or 5 sessions the staff member in charge of the class turned to me and asked me if I would like to respond. I nodded in the affirmative and began to write my response. After about 20 minutes I formulated my response and handed it to her where she read it quietly before reading it aloud to the class.

After a few minutes she turned and looked at me and said to the class, "I have just read what Randall has written, and I am amazed to say the least. For I have gone to college for years to obtain my PHD in human psychology and to learn the things that he has written down on paper before me today.

Not only has he written about the cause and effect of the human condition but he goes on to say that there is but only one answer to our emotional, spiritual and mental issues in this life. I take great honor to read in his behalf what he has written this day. And she began to read to the class how I see God working in our lives and the ways that He goes about bringing us into His love.

Once again, the Lord, had brought his people to hear His Word.

__As the heavens are higher than the earth__
__so are my ways higher than your ways__
__and my thoughts are higher than yours.__
__Isaiah 55:9__

Here I was in a mental hospital, the last place I thought I would ever find myself and doing the last thing I thought I would be doing in such a place. I was testifying...

I was testifying about the love of my Father in heaven.

There were many days when the sterile clinical approach to mental our issues were being address by other staff members according to their book. One morning the staff member that was overseeing our class was called away on an emergency leaving the dry erasure board covered with words that I knew would never bring life. So I went up in front of the class and wiped the board clean and began to write some things from my heart. When I had finished I turned to see that everyone there had been feverously writing down every word I had written. For I had written again about the love of God for his people and the ways that He goes about revealing that love to them.

Before I left Parkway Medical Center I had many of those that sat there that day come up to me and write in my spiral note book thank you notes and blessings for the words that I wrote that day. These were people that were severely brokenhearted and mentally disturbed yet they were touched that day by the love of God and they will remember that day forever... as I surely will...

I still own that spiral notebook to this date.

His ways and His thoughts are surely above ours.

Many years before my time at Parkway I remembered a sermon that Pastor Chuck preached on the revelation of God. The sermon had at its base the following:

Revelation brings Confrontation…

Confrontation brings Assimilation…

Years later I would add and Assimilation brings son ship.

For God is able to make all things, all the chaos, all the crisis in our lives, to an expected end.

And that end, is to be found in Christ Jesus.

O, how wonderful it is to be found in the beloved!

This is the pattern that we will experience if we walk the path of God seeking the person of the truth, Christ Jesus.

I was submerged deep in the confrontation stage in my own mind and I had to still come to a place where assimilation would became a wheel that would move me down the path of God with ever gathering speed.

Line upon line and precept upon precept was being laid in my heart as I moved in the Word of God. The love of God was abiding in me and I was growing in the truth that I was His son. I was receiving and abiding in the perfect love of the Only Begotten Son of God Almighty. And His Name is Christ Jesus.

For Jesus Christ my solid rock.

He is the rock of my salvation.

Chapter 18

LOVE SONG

I left Parkway and the divorce went through just as I had expected. I was soon homeless without a job and still unable to speak a single word. But the Lord looked down from on high and had mercy on my dilemma and provided a safe place for me off Claremont Road not too many miles from the church I was attending. My ex-wife filed a petition with Social Security without my knowing and I started receiving SSI which helped pay the $450.00 a month rent. I had no cell phone or car, my mother would drive up from Fayetteville Georgia to take me to Grady for my surgeries. To communicate with her I would call her from a phone and after having had established a code, I would have her ask questions and I would respond with one tone for yes and 2 tones for no. A brother in the Lord from Christ Fellowship gave me an old IBM computer where I learned the DOS operating system. And I started writing down my experiences with the Lord and what would later become what you reading as my first book. Little did I know that this had been His perfect will all along? It was late in 1993 and I was fast away writing down all the things that I had experienced with the Lord on my journey. As I wrote those words on paper I began to realize that my life was being used by God to show his faithfulness and loving-kindness to his people. He had chosen someone like me. I knew that I didn't deserve His attention and yet despite all my failures He commended his everlasting love towards me daily and He would never resend it. I knew that beyond a shadow of a doubt that I belonged to God and nothing could change that truth. ***For who am I that the God of the universe is mindful of me?*** I now knew the reason that I had been born and now I had a reason to live. I was living out the word of Dr. McCluen who came to visit me. <u>Randall, this is not unto death! You will recover and serve the Lord.</u>

I felt that I was in days of walking out all the things that God had planned for me. For His loving-kindness and mercy had brought me full circle back to those directives that He gave me that morning on Lacy Street many years before. Through all my bad decisions, rebellion and stupidity, He had taken those things and fashioned them for my good. He had kept his word and he had kept me. For He is a God that cannot lie. He had made me an example of his patience, longsuffering and his great love. I was coming home to my Father's house where he was waiting on me with open arms. One night after writing an article on sexual defilement I was awakened just before dawn with the sounds of someone singing over me. Someone was standing beside my bed singing words that I could not understand. Those words were so beautiful that all I could do was lay there and weep with joy as He bathed me in His song of love. To this date I have never heard such sounds again, but I knew that morning that this was God singing his love song over me. I did not see Him with my natural eyes but I was made aware in my spirit that it was the Lord. How can we not want to know such a God? How can we not want to receive such a love as this? How can we reject this all-consuming love? How can we turn away from the lover of our soul?

__Jesus, you are the lover of my soul.__
__Lord, I love you and adore you, what more can I say.__
__Lord, you cause my love for you to grow stronger every day.__

Chapter 19

I CAN SEE

Although I did not understand the language of those words that morning the experience encouraged me to move forward with Godspeed to finish my surgeries. I worked out a deal with my ex-wife and I got the VW rabbit we had during the marriage even though I still had double and triple vision. I at least had a car to drive when I got my vision back.

One Wednesday evening Greg Wood came by and picked me up to go to church. As I sat on the back row I felt as though I was supposed to go up front and hug Pastor Chuck as he took up the evening offering. Greg had to help me down the aisle as I could not walk without falling. Pastor Chuck was standing in the middle of the floor as I walked up and put my arms around him squeezed him tightly but ever so gently as not to break a rib. It was just as I hugged him that I felt what I can only describe as a jolt of electricity pass through him into me. It was a very intense shock that went into my very being and it seemed that I had been the only one aware of the experience. I went back to my seat and 3 days later I woke up and my eyes had locked on and my vision had been completely restored. I had 20/20 vision. I went to the hospital and the doctors tested me and could not believe their eyes. They had given up on my vision having done everything in their power, and yet there I stood before them healed again by the power of God. Now I could drive myself to the hospital for my surgeries. Although I had been blind now I could see. I believe that this was yet another sign from God as he was continuing to make me an example of his love. Notwithstanding, I also believe that it had in no small measure something to do with the respect and love that I have for the first man to ever speak living words into my being all those years ago.

Relationships are very important to God, and I had a deep abiding relationship with this man. He was the first human being that I loved with the love of God. *''I will be forever grateful that he heard the call from God and answered and by the grace of God our paths would cross on that Wednesday night. For God used him to release my soul and place my feet on the path of God and my destiny.*

A night designed by God himself.

I would drive myself to Grady Hospital check myself in on Wednesday and have major surgery on Thursday and check myself out on Friday and be back at work on Monday morning. This was the ever growing level of the grace of God on my life. I was working with Greg Wood helping him on his painting jobs. I would sweep floors and pick up trash as I only had $50.00 left after paying my rent. I also worked for Jeff Benoit helping him clean a hair salon in Buckhead at nights. I would scrub floors and sweep up hair while listening to my worship music on tape. Once I started working I called the Social Security Administration and canceled my benefits and told them that I was going to start my own company. This was the only work that I could find to pay my child support. After all, I was walking medical experiment in recovery.

I was having car trouble with the VW and Greg helped me get an old Chrysler Cordoba in exchange for painting a 200 foot shed. The car had been sitting for a very long time and it needed a lot of work. I knew it needed a tune so I had bought the parts and was going to install them on Friday after Thanksgiving. The hair salon was on Peachtree Street in down-town Atlanta and I wanted to get home before the parades got started.

So around 6am I went and loaded up to leave and jumped into the car but it would not start. So I decided to put in the spark plugs figuring that it would be a simple job. I got 7 plugs out but the eight one would not come out no matter what I did. Finally, in frustration I broke it off only to find out that someone had crossed threaded it in a previous tune up. I became very angry and started hitting the fender with the wrench screaming at God through my surgical mask, **"After *all that I have gone through and after all that I have suffered and even though I believe that I am your son, all you have given to me is junk!*

*Nothing but other people's problems!***

After I had calmed down I heard that gentle voice that I had heard so many times before.

And He said, ***and what have you given to me my son?***

All this took place on Thanksgiving Day and in looking back it could not have happened on a more appropriate day to reveal to me that I still had some very important elements to develop in my relationship with the Lord. The foundational truth about thanksgiving, praise and worship would have to come front and center if I was to ever mature spiritually in Christ Jesus.

For the Spirit of the Lord goes to and fro throughout the earth seeking those whose hearts are perfect towards Him in spirit and truth and those that worship Him must worship in spirit and in truth.

Yes I had poured my heart to him many times and I had even danced before in the mountains, I even sang songs to him from my heart, but I had not understood the importance of Worship, Praise and Thanksgiving as a daily sacrifice in my life.

Chapter 20

PRAISE AND THANKSGIVING

I had to come to the place where when I found myself in trouble or needy, I would will myself to worship and praise the Lord. From this place I would receive strength and encouragement from on high to continue onto my destiny in Christ Jesus.

Worship had to become one of the most important building blocks in my life. Without worship and praise I could never expect to have the reality of God. From that Thanksgiving Day forward I knew that I could not do anything that would bring Him the glory, honour and praise He deserves unless I became a true worshipper.

Moreover, the rich storehouse of His blessings would remain locked up in heaven. Worship in spirit and truth releases the blessings of God into our lives and we are healed from all that the enemy has robbed from us.

Years ago the Blessed Holy Spirit said, ***"Today, I give unto you the keys of the Kingdom of Heaven."***

I now knew what those words meant and if I was to ever bring God pleasure, I would have to embrace worship, praise, the singing of songs and dancing before Him and incorporate them as a life-style. I would go to the hospital for my surgery date and instead of taking the elevators I would run up 6-7-8 flights of stairs praising my God the entire way. Thanking him for healing me and healing my vision and for giving me the strength to complete my surgeries. I would leave my appointments and run back down as fast as I could singing songs from my heart thanking Him for keeping me on the path to my calling.

I would continue to write articles as I was moved by the Holy Spirit while worshipping God the whole time. Many times my heart would break before Him and the experience would be so intense that all I could do was sit there and weep. For I know beyond a shadow of a doubt that I am not worthy to write these words let alone to even gaze upon their beauty. Yet in his loving- kindness and everlasting mercy towards me, His passion draws near to me. He continues to reveal himself to me daily.

He is closer to me than a brother.

For where can I go that His Holy Spirit is not there.

If I make my bed in hell surely you are there with me.

"For the eyes of the Lord run to and fro throughout the whole earth, to show

himself strong on the behalf of those whose heart is loyal to him.
And again, "Yet a time is coming and now has come when the true worshippers will worship the Father in spirit and in truth, for they are the kind of worshippers that the Father seeks.
God is spirit, and his worshippers must worship in spirit and truth." John 4:23-24

And I was becoming one of those that He desires.

The Kingdom of Heaven was being opened before me through worship and praise and my paths were being ordered and they led me to Doctor James A. Davis. This man blessed me with dental work, implants and a prosthetic nose so that I could get out from behind the blue surgical mask that I had worn for years.

In exchange for his help Chris Adams and I enclosed his basement addition in Jonesboro. Doctor Davis spent his off time talking to other doctors that he knew to see if they would do work on my case pro bono. Through Dr. Davis, I was introduced to Dr. Steven Cohen at Atlanta Plastic Medical Center in Dunwoody Georgia. Dr. Cohen would use all of his God given talents to finish what the doctors at Grady, Northside, Saint Joseph, Shallowford hospitals had begun.

I will be eternally grateful for all that Dr. Davis has done for me. I know that I can never repay him for all that he has done for me. And the same can be said for all the doctors that poured their hearts and souls into my recovery and reconstruction.

I ask my Father in heaven to pour out on each one of them a very special blessing. In Jesus Christ Name

I moved out of the bi weekly motel into a 2 bedroom duplex in Mableton Ga. and continued to work with Greg Wood and his painting company. Greg would tell his customers that he had someone that could do the repairs and he would schedule the job for me.

I took the back seat out of my VW and loaded it with tools. I tied my ladders on top and went to pawn shops to buy my tools to work. I would go out and do a job never saying a word to the customer. I worked my surgeries around my contract work never missing a beat.

I was still unable to speak one audible word but that was about to change. One night I took a full length mirror and placed in front of me and sat down on the couch. I began to pray in the spirit and thank God for all that He had done for me. Then I moved over into prophesying and declaring those things that are not as though they were.

I would sit there night after night and point my finger at the image that I did not recognize in the mirror. I would declare from my heart making inaudible gurgling sounds that one day very soon I would shout the glories of the Lord. I would prophesy that a day would soon dawn that I would be able to speak so that all those that had ears to hear with would hear of the great and mighty things my God has done for me.

As I had additional operations on my mouth the doctors would have to cut and split my jaw, install steel plates and screws. Each time they did this procedure I would have to go home and start trying to speak all over again. I would have to try and say my abc's each and every time. I went over 5 and one half years without speaking one audible word. And by the grace of God I taught my-self to speak again even though every doctor I had met said that I would never speak again.

This went on for months until I began to understand with my own ears the sounds that I was making. I knew that by the Spirit I was well on my way to recovery and moreover, I was still holding onto my Father's promise that this would not end in death. But I would recover and serve Him. Sitting in front of that mirror day after day I had encouraged myself spiritually, so much so that I was ready to step out into deeper waters. The very same waters that I had ran from years before.

Chapter 21

DEEP WATERS

I started my own company and used most of the money that I made to buy upgraded equipment for my budding business. At first it was very difficult because I was still very self-conscience of my disfigurement. I still wore the surgical mask and I was unable to eat any solid food. To eat I would have to use an extra-large syringe and pump fluid into my stomach. I had a trach tube sticking out of my throat but that didn't stop me from going out and doing 3 story roof repairs. I also did concrete/ fence/ and anything related to home repairs. Having not ever done many of these things I would go to Home Depot and buy how to books then go out solicit jobs. I continued to worship God in spirit and in truth and my strength continued to grow and the muscle that I had lost was returning.

I was being renewed day by day.

Psalms 103:1-5 Praise the Lord, O my soul, all my inmost being, praise his holy name. Praise the Lord, O my soul, and forget not all his benefits who forgives all your sins and heals all your diseases, who redeems your life from the pit and crowns you with love and compassion, who satisfies you your desires with good things so that your youth is renewed like the eagle's.

I asked the Lord if he knew of anyone that needed to be blessed and that I would like to be used to help that person. Shortly after this prayer He sent me to a widow woman who was living in a trailer park over in Douglasville Georgia. Her trailer was literally falling apart from the floors to the electrical and water.

This old woman had to sleep holding onto a baseball bat while wearing a football helmet because of the possums and rats that ran up and down the halls through her trailer at night. I gathered some brothers together and we went to rebuild her home. John Edwards and I installed new water lines as the ones that were there were so corroded and filled with metal shavings it was impossible for water to flow through them.

Greg bought her a new stove and I gave her some new furniture and clothes. Chris Adams and I sealed her trailer roof among a lot of other repairs. While Greg and I were working on her trailer one day she came out and said that she had been praying for us and specifically praying for me. She said the Lord had told her to begin to prophesy a wife for me and that she would be coming right soon.

I retorted, **NO THANKS!**

On paper as I carried some with me everywhere.

That word ain't for me! Give that word to Greg he's never been married and wants to be married in a real bad way. Let him get a taste of marriage! But I will not go down that road again! After all my problems with my last marriage I wanted nothing to do with a new relationship with another woman period!

The widow woman said, well I have been instructed by the Lord to prophesy over you and prophesy over you I shall!

I covered my ears as she began to speak, for in my heart I wanted nothing to do with that word. Yet, this was an area that the Lord wanted to heal in me but I was not willing to allow him access. I would have never prayed that prayer if I had the slightest inclination that that subject would have come to the surface.

A few days later Greg bought me a new computer with windows the first version. I could now write my articles and do work on flyers for our businesses. The very day that we brought the system home we signed up for AOL just as the internet craze was getting started. I got online and found myself in a chat room with a bunch of married and divorced people discussing their issues.

The conversation came around to me and I was asked how I felt about marriage. So I launched off into a tirade of all the disappointments that I had with my previous relationship. When I was finished someone by the screen name of Linda responded rather angrily asking me, who do you think you are to say such things about marriage?

I retorted, "If you had gone through the things that I just went through you might feel the same way." Little did I know that this conversation would be the beginning of something that would sneak up on me and overwhelm me? We started sending emails to each other and I told her everything about my life and that I had attempted suicide many times. I basically used this time to witness about the Lord and the things that He had done for me. I had absolutely no intention whatsoever of entering into a new relationship with anyone. We used the internet for several months before we used the phone as I was still relearning how to speak all over again. During this time Linda told me about herself and that she was in the metals industry specifically the aluminum field. She told me that she had a BA in metallurgy and worked for Kaiser Aluminum in Ca. When I heard this information I thought, why any woman with her education would want to have a relationship with someone like me. I didn't even finish high school.

Chapter 22

RELEASE THE HOUNDS

Linda, told me that from time to time her company would send her out of the country to do analysis on different plants within their industry and that this was one of those times. She had been asked to fly to Bolivia and take a jeep deep into the jungle to inspect the quality and control department. She said that she might be able to email depending on the system there at the plant in South America.

With all that I had just gone through in my life I had a hard time swallowing this information. I had already heard about the many scams and practical jokes being played on people on the internet by college kids. I said, sure you are. When you get there make sure you send me an email. Hahaaha

I had no way of knowing that I was emailing a real woman much less someone who was legitimate in the metal industry. I continued to communicate with her for several more months before we actually spoke on the phone. For all I knew a group of college guys had put some poor girl up to calling me. I had thoughts about a bunch of college guys laughing themselves right in the emergency room because they had a real live idiot online in Atlanta. Finally, the day came that we would talk on the phone so I asked Linda by email if she wanted to call me and she agreed. Even with her on the phone I was not convinced that she was for real. We spoke on the phone for several months the best I could speak anyway. She asked if I would like to come out to CA. and meet her in person. I said, sure I am game.

Linda sent me a ticket and I soon found myself headed to Ca. to meet a woman that I had never seen not even in a picture. Neither of us had exchanged pictures during this entire time. Before I left for California I bought 2 dozen long stem red roses and had them wrapped and boxed just in case this wasn't a joke and she was for real. I remember sitting on the runway in Atlanta thinking to myself, "boy randy, you have done some pretty stupid things in your life, but this one may take the cake and the candles to boot.

This would be the farthest west I had ever been and the longest plane ride of my life. Upon my arrival at SFO we were told that all the non-international gates were full and we would be deplaning at an international gate. Linda had instructed me that when I arrive to wait for her that she would meet at the gate.

I asked, how will I recognize you? She said I have red hair and green eyes. So when I deplaned I stood where I had been instructed to stand holding a box of

2 dozen roses wearing a blue surgical mask waiting for a red headed woman with green eyes to appear.

Boy, did I felt like one big fool!

I thought to myself, well if this is a joke at least I had a free round trip ticket and with that I might be able to deal with the humiliation of this whole ordeal.

I waited for quite some time and wouldn't you know the airport was filled with red headed women with green eyes. Finally after about 30 minutes I thought that I heard my name being called over the intercom. After a second time I wandered up to a customer service desk and wrote down on paper, did you just call for Randall Rogers?

I was told that the party that was supposed to meet me had been held up at security as non-passengers were not allowed to come into the international area. The attendant directed me towards the security gate which was a 10 minute walk. I started up the concourse still not knowing whom or what I was going to meet. As I passed through the security gate I was blindsided and nearly knocked to the floor. The next thing I knew someone had their arms around me and I was being smothered in kisses.

It was Linda! And I never saw her coming!

And to my relief she was a woman to boot!

God had fulfilled His word that the old widow woman had prophesied over my covered ears. His goodness and mercy had chased me down and overwhelmed me. We spent the next few weeks driving all over CA. from the mountains to the beach.

Linda drove me down to Monterey and we had lunch at Clint Eastwood's restaurant. Linda ate lunch

I just sat there and took in the scenery. On the way back we stopped along Hwy 1 where we went out on the beach and laid down a blanket and I held her in my arms as we watched the sun set over the Pacific Ocean. I knew that the Lord had brought me my soul mate and He blessed me abundantly. The Lord had put His love in this woman's heart to love me sight unseen even though I had resisted the Lord, He had blessed me with someone that could overlook my disfigurement and see my heart and love me.

His Banner over me is Love! His Banner over me is Love!

I could see His hands all over this relationship and I knew that I would never be alone again. Once again, I had someone in my life that loved me and wanted me. I was special to her and she was special to me.

Each time I looked at her I could see the love of God for me in her eyes. I knew from the bottom of my heart that He had chosen her to help me reach my destiny. For it is vitally important that a man have a helpmate that is in agreement with him. It is the most powerful union in the earth. After I arrived back home my phone bill went from $30.00 a month the over $400.00 a month and giving the fact that my rent was only $400.00 a month something had to be done. Financially, I knew that things were going to have to change if this relationship was going to continue. We both logged quite a few frequent flyer miles before deciding that maybe this long distance relationship would be better served in one location.

We decided to make a lifelong commitment to each and entered into a covenant before the Lord. I flew out and got Linda and brought her back to Atlanta. Greg Wood's uncle ***just happened*** to have a house for sale in Marietta and ***just happened*** to have a VW Vanagon for sale. I was having trouble with my VW rabbit and it was in need serious repair. And besides I wanted a newer model anyway.

I had given the old widow woman the car that Greg had given me in one of my many trips to work on her trailer before my trip to Ca. Her only means of transportation had been walking to the bus or getting rides from friends. After giving her the car she told me that she was going to pray that God would bless me with a brand new truck for my new business and for blessing her with all the things that she needed. I thought that the Vanagon was the answer to that prayer.

We bought the house and I helped Linda get all of her things from Ca. and Ohio to Atlanta. Linda was hired to work in the Lab at Lockheed Martin Aeronautical in Marietta. This was an answer to prayer also.

Linda encouraged me to step out into even deeper waters with God for my business and to believe God for even greater success. She would come home from Lockheed after having been up since 5am and help me make and distribute flyers in the evenings in the communities in around where we lived.

It was Linda's idea to name the company Honey-Do and I added the Homes Services Inc.

And, Honey-Do Home Services was born.

And the work came in like a flood and I had more than I could by myself. I had to farm some of it out to Greg, John, Chris and many others. I quickly outgrew my VW Vanagon and the little trailer that I pulled behind. I went back to the widow woman and told her what had happened with her prophesy over me about a wife, she was so blessed and encouraged that she prayed in the spirit right there over me asking God to do something special with regards to a new truck.

Within a couple of weeks I found myself in a Ford Lincoln Mercury Dealership looking at the new Lincoln Navigators. As I stood there I could not believe that I was even contemplating such a thing, and the truth was I was very nervous. So I decided on the one that I wanted only to find out that I would have to order it and it would take several weeks. I looked and saw the same one on the showroom floor and asked if I could have that one instead. I was told yes. And so, I drove a brand new Lincoln Navigator off the showroom floor.

I stopped the Navigator just down the road and wept giving thanks to God who had turned my life around.

This was the most expensive vehicle that I had ever owned and it was loaded with all the bells and whistles it cost over $50,000. I was living in a $225,000 home pulling a trailer with over $80,000 worth of tools for my business. And standing beside me was my helpmate chosen by the very hand of Almighty God.

I was no longer driving junk cars.

I was no longer homeless.

I was no longer alone.

My chaos and all my crisis's had brought me to Christ and the Kingdom of God had come in my life. My Father in heaven had led me by his Holy Spirit to the place that He desired for me to be in His Son.

I have experienced great darkness in my soul and great pain, as I was called to walk the valley so that God might reveal himself to me in the manner in which He chose. Years ago in Buckhead I would cry out to Him and to him alone and ask, Father God, I want to know you as no other man before. ***And He answered, you shall my son. For there has never been one like you.***

We are all created different for different purposes in the earth. For each of us have a special signature sealed in the Blood of Christ. I had to walk through the valley of the shadow of death so that when I came out the other side I would know my God and my Creator. In death I had been born again and in darkness my eyes had seen the glorious light of this all knowing, all merciful and all loving God. Had I not gone down that path I would not be able to sit here and tell you of the patience, longsuffering and ever-lasting amazing love of this God that has revealed himself to me in a very deep and profound way.

Chaos… to Crisis… to Christ, my Lord, my King, my God and my friend.

This ancient truth has become flesh of my flesh and bone of my bone. Yes, a living reality to His existence and mighty power and everlasting love. I have become a living believer by His grace and mercy. I have become a new creature in Christ Jesus, for old things have passed away and all things have become new. I have become a living worshipper.

This truth has become firmly established on the bedrock of my soul as a sure foundation. My God loves me and I love Him with all my heart and nothing and no one can ever remove me from that place and remove me from His loving arms. I am sure that I will have many more trials to walk through in this life, but the one thing that I will hold onto to for dear life, is that I know God and I know his love for me. And I am no longer a loser. I am no longer afraid of failure. I have embraced my failures and with faith in God he has changed me into a success. And I am worthy to belong to God because His Word says that I am. I will continue to hold onto His mighty hand until I see Him at his Kingdom gates. This then is my story about the love of God and how He went about revealing himself to me and making me His son. My journey started when I was 7years old and today I turn 58 years old.

For He said, many years ago, I am going to make you an example of my patience, longsuffering and my love. I am going to make you an example of my patience, longsuffering and my love to my people

and they will know that, "I am the Lord thy God."

He is faithful to see that his word does not return to him void but accomplishes the purpose for which it was sent...
I love Him with all my heart, soul, mind and strength...

John 10:27-30
My sheep listen to my voice; I know them and they follow me. I give them eternal life and they shall not perish; No one can snatch them out of my hand. My Father, who has given them to me, is greater than all; no one can snatch them out of my Father's hand. I and the Father are one.

It is my heart felt prayer that if you were touched by the reading of these simple words that you open your mouth and say out loud, asking the God that I know that He would come into your life with power and love in Christ Jesus name.

For I have tasted of the Lord's great love and His peace that surpasses all understanding. For my Father is no respecter of persons for what He has done for me He will most certainly do for you.

For He has kept me.
For He has healed me.
For He has blessed me.

For He has filled me to overflowing with His Mighty Holy Presence.
For He has filled me with his amazing love
For He has made me free to love Him and to Honor Him and to Worship Him in spirit and in truth.
He has made me His son.
He has made me an example to you...
And He is waiting for you...

In Closing I want to pray for this Nation and her peoples.

Father God, in the Holy name of Christ Jesus hear my petition, hear my cry, hear my plea and let my words come before your Holy throne.

O Ancient One, I cry out to you from the bottom of my heart look upon me and receive this prayer.

I confess the sins of our nation that we have turned our backs on your Holy Word. I confess that we have treated your Holy sacrifice with scorn and contempt. I confess that we are no longer a house of prayer and we have robbed you of all that you deserve. I confess that we have turned our hearts away from you to follow after other gods. O Lord, do not forget nor cast away the nation that you established by your grace for your purpose in the earth. I confess that we have sinned against you and you alone have we sinned.

We are a nation that no longer fears your Holy Name.

The nations of world mock us even now, asking where is there God?

O Great and Mighty One of Israel, do not let us be destroyed along with the unbelievers in the earth.

Save a remnant for yourself! Pour out upon us your precious Holy Spirit and cleanse us that we might return unto you with all of our heart.

Reveal yourself to your people as you have revealed yourself to me,

O God of Israel. Do not allow this nation to be destroyed! Give us one more chance to confess our sins and return to our first love.

Save Christ Jesus.

O God Most High, I cry out to you from the bottom of my being! Let the place where we live become the house of prayer and let our prayers reach your ears. I ask that you answer quickly for even now our enemies are at the door.

I cry out to you to come and be with those that love you and honour your holy name.

O Ancient One, take for yourself a tithe of all that is upon the earth and that belongs to you for your Glory.

O Ancient One, arise and come and show yourself mighty in our behalf and let revival break throughout in this land.

For your Glory, Honour and Praise.

Let this be the generation that lifts up your Holy Name and let your glorious light shine upon your people.

O Lord, come quickly in great power and vindicate your Holy Name.

O Lord, glorify your Only Begotten Son in the earth.

O Lord God, turn this curse away from our land.

In Christ Jesus Name I cry, I pray...Save your people...

O Lord God most high, let your amazing begin to pour forth like a mighty river upon this dry and barren nation.

For your name's sake come and save your people.

Amen

EPILOGUE

There is no end to the writing of books… and so it is with me.

Since I finished this book there has been even more experiences with the Lord, so much so that a second and possibly a third book is in the offing. My life continues to be an open book and the chapters that the Lord wants to author are far from complete.

If you would like to contact me please email me, @ **randall.rogers98@yahoo.com**

Or you can snail mail me @
Randall H. Rogers
190 Turkey Point Drive
Lagrange, Georgia. 30240
May the God of Israel bless you till you overflow with His Holy presence.

September 10th 2014

Zulon Publishers, The following is the closing author's back page for "Chaos... to Crisis... To Christ!" containing the 300 word minimum that you requested. I sincerely hope that this will finalize the book and get it over to the printers as soon as possible. I have received many requests for the book even before it goes to the printers and the excitement is high to say the least. I believe that this book will become a best seller and your printers will have a very hard time keeping up with demand. I believe the Lord will soon be blessed with the words that are contained in this simple and childlike book.

Please help me finish this book as it has been a very hard trial getting it to this point. The enemy knows that many of God's people will be ministered to and receive healing from above to the glory and honor and praise of almighty God. With everything that I have experienced in my life as written in the book, writing this book and getting it into the hands of those that are dying without Christ Jesus even as I write, has been the hardest thing in my life to accomplish. I am exhausted mentally and physically to the point I have thought of just throwing it on the shelf and walking away. But praise His holy name He has given me his grace to go just a little further and to see it through to the end, and so here I am.

The Author of the book, "Chaos to... Crisis... To Christ!" presently resides in Lagrange Georgia on seventy acres of land where they rent a modest home overlooking a 4 acre stocked lake. Randall is accompanied by his lifelong partner Linda K. Kern who presently suffers from MS and other medical issues and he has been her only care provider during her lengthy illness. They have been together for nearly 20 years. She is a graduate of Kennedy Western University with Bachelor of Science in Quality Management and received her Master's in Human Resource Management. The old adage about opposites attract is no truer here. In their nearly twenty years together Linda has been a well spring of encouragement to him. They are more than just a married couple in the eyes of the Lord, they have also become best friends and they are in spiritual agreement across the board touching the call of God upon Randall's life. Randall failed to finish high school but having said that, his life has been anything but a complete failure. His life is rich beyond imagination with untold experiences with the awesome power, mercy and love of the One and Only true God. Save Christ Jesus. It is this same awesome power that has kept him through all his chaos and crisis's and blessed him and kept him from certain death many times, and now causes him to stand upon the Rock of our salvation, even at this late hour so that this book might be placed in the hands of God's people.

Whenever the opportunity presents itself you will find the author on the lake fishing with his Lord. As it is written in the book he loves to bass fish. For it was the fishing trip to Lake June Aluska North Carolina that put his feet securely on the path to the Kingdom of our God. While on the lake Randall finds the peace and tranquility necessary to continue to move forward with his vision for the property and to finish the calling on his life. After 40 years of depression and darkness Randall has been healed in his mind and given the power to dream the things of God. It is his heartfelt desire and continual prayer before the Lord, that the perfect will of God be done in his life and somehow through the simple words of this book help those that struggle with the doubt and unbelief about the love and kindness and mercy of the God that he serves. He believes that this simple book will inspire and encourage many of God's children to dig down deep and seek Him, who alone can change a human heart and fill the void within with His amazing love. For the hour of his return is at the door.

The day will soon dawn where those that come to this place will pass underneath a banner that proclaims,

"His Banner over us is His amazing love."

For without His amazing love flowing through us and covering us we are nothing more than cymbals making noise.

This then is my story, for I am an open book to be read by all men.

I have been written as an example to you with the experiences of God in my body so that all who read my story will know that He is,

"The Lord thy God"

Jesus, I love you with all my heart.
I place all my dreams and desires in your hands.
For you are my God.
For you are my King.
And you are my friend.
I pray for all those that read these words.
Touch them as you have touched me.
"I am my beloveds and He is mine!"

CPSIA information can be obtained at www.ICGtesting.com
Printed in the USA
LVOW04s1145070115

421806LV00019B/163/P